UNDER SYDENHAM SKIES

A CELEBRATION OF COUNTRY LIFE

CORNELIA JOHANNA BAINES

Fitzhenry & Whiteside

Under Sydenham Skies

Fitzhenry and Whiteside Limited
195 Allstate Parkway
Markham, Ontario L3R 4T8

In the United States:
121 Harvard Avenue, Suite 2
Allston, Massachusetts 02134

www.fitzhenry.ca godwit@fitzhenry.ca

Fitzhenry & Whiteside acknowledges with thanks the Canada Council
for the Arts, the Government of Canada through its Book Publishing Industry
Development Program, and the Ontario Arts Council for their support
of our publishing program.

Canadian Cataloguing in Publication Data

Baines, Cornelia Johanna
 Under Sydenham skies: a celebration of country life

ISBN 1-55041-615-4

1. Country life - Ontario - Sydenham. 2. Sydenham (Ont.) - History.
3. Sydenham (Ont.) - Social life and customs. I. Title.

FC3099.S93A39 2000 971.3,71 C00-932560-3
F1059.5.S93B34 2000

Design: Darrell McCalla

Photographs not otherwise attributed are by the author.

Printed and bound in Canada

In memory of my mother, Lottie Van Erk
In tribute to my husband, Andrew
And a story for our children, grandchildren
and whoever follows.

Cornelia Baines and her husband Andrew are seen in their garden at the Hougues Magues. Over a period of three decades, it has been enjoyed by four generations of their family.

Photo By Michael McLuhan MPA.

Contents

Recipes from the Hougues Magues

Recipes from the
Hougues Magues

List of Photographs and Illustrations

Preface

Every book is, in an intimate sense,
a circular letter to the friends of (her) who writes it.

Robert Louis Stevenson in a letter to Sidney Colvin.
Quoted in *Travels with a Donkey in the Cevennes* (1879). Marlboro Press.
Northwestern University Press. Evanston Ill. 1996

THIS IS A PERSONAL STORY based on memories of what my family has done, seen and been told, memories related to one special farm, nestled in the Bighead Valley, near the village of Bognor in the Township of Sydenham. Telling such a story invades privacy, ours, and that of the people I write about, those we have known in the past three decades, and those who were there long ago. I hope my story will yield pleasure and offend no one.

In his book *The Old Way of Seeing Things: How Architecture Lost Its Magic (And How To Get It Back)*, Jonathon Hale writes about "therelessness." He believes that in the past, designers of buildings succeeded in contrast to those of today, because they saw "pattern in light and shade" and, using intuition achieved proportion. Without this intuition, without proportion, without pattern, many of the buildings of today are dull, mismatched, uncertain. Hale describes this as anomie, "therelessness." For me, that captures precisely what distinguishes most contemporary residential architecture, especially in suburban subdivisions, from the beautiful house this book describes, a building whose character, whose "thereness" stands out, even from a distance.

When I began writing on July 6, 1999, I didn't know whether I was writing for me, or for my family, or for Sydenham residents, or for a wider audience. Nor had I remembered that the Township of Sydenham celebrates its 150th anniversary in the year 2000 even though it is about to be arbitrarily amalgamated out of existence. Then I came to realize that this book is, as Robert Louis Stevenson wrote, a letter to my friends—and who knows how far flung they will be. Within another ten years, all first-hand memories about people who began their lives in the mid-1800s will have gone. That is one of many reasons for writing. Another is to share recipes, including many from Sydenham. However, the most important reason is to celebrate and sing the praises of the Bighead Valley (the Queen's Valley as it used to be called in honour of Queen Victoria), to remember the achievements of the first settlers, and to marvel at what is to be found under Sydenham skies.

Toronto 2000

IN THE BEGINNING

Chapter I

Serendipity

Serendipity: *The faculty of happening upon fortunate discoveries*
when not in search of them.

Funk & Wagnalls Canadian College Dictionary.

E STOPPED THE CAR at the top of the hill. My mother and I got
out. Stretching southwards and to the east lay the Queen's
Valley, rich in the colours of early autumn. On either side of
the Bighead River, an undulating patchwork of luminous fields spread
out across the valley floor. Off in the distant horizon were "the Blue
Mountains," or at the least (so I thought), their foothills. Completely
hidden was the village of Bognor which lay just one concession east of
us. To the north, beyond our sight, lay Georgian Bay.

Fred Miller had driven us here to show us his house which was
up for sale. There it was. Below us, in a smaller valley between where
we stood and a hill to the east of us, was an "Ontario vernacular," one-
and-a-half storied centre-plan stone house. Framing the front door
were sidelights and a transom window, and above the front door were
a gable and a gothic window. Although it could not be seen from the
road, the house had the traditional kitchen ell at the rear. Similar
houses, stone, brick or wood-frame, can be seen all over Southern

Ontario. Here in Grey County in the Township of Sydenham, in the last quarter of the 19th century, many such houses were built of local stone by Scottish immigrants.

"How much are you asking?" I said. We were still standing by the car. When I heard the price, my response was instantaneous. I think I remember my mother gasping as I said "We'll buy it." I knew without any doubt at all that Andrew would agree.

<hr>

BY THE SPRING of 1970, Andrew and I had to face the fact that we and our two children, Nickie and Nigel, then aged 12 and 7, could no longer continue to enjoy exclusive use of the family cottage on Caledon Lake which had been such an important part of our lives for so long. When Andrew's father retired, the rather small cottage on the rather small lake simply could not accommodate three generations with conflicting lifestyles. Rising at 6 a.m. and dining at 5.30 p.m. was not for us.

So that summer we did not spend our vacation at Caledon Lake; Nickie went to stay with friends in France and we went camping with Nigel and a young friend. Our destination was the North Shore of Lake Superior, the most grand and spectacular of the five Great Lakes which separate the USA and Canada. That camping trip made us aware as never before, just how enormous our province of Ontario is. In the mid-sixties we had lived in North Carolina for two years. That had been a 14-hour drive south from Toronto into a radically differ-ent climate and culture. In 1970 we drove 14 hours north and west of Toronto, at which point we were still far from Ontario's western bor-der with Manitoba, and we were just under half way to Ontario's northernmost boundary. Not only were we still in our own country, we were still in our own province. A huge land!

Our summer expedition was idyllic. The weather was perfect and the scenery spectacular. The campsites were spacious and well-groomed. Blueberries were everywhere—densely blue, sweet, plump and firm, and so closely bunched on the low bushes that you could pick them by the handful. Fish were so obligingly catchable it was difficult not to haul in more than we could eat. We pan-fried them in butter over our campfire. They were so delicious that even the two boys ate them with gusto night after night.

Our route to the North Shore had taken us along the east shore of Georgian Bay. For our return trip, we drove across Manitoulin Island and picked up the ferry that goes from South Bay Mouth on the south side of the island to Tobermory at the north end of the Bruce Peninsula. From Tobermory (pronounced "Tubbermory" locally) south to Toronto was a five-hour drive.

All went well until we found ourselves in downtown Owen Sound where we got stuck in a traffic jam. So slow was the traffic that I was able to escape briefly from our hot car and look at a window display of properties for sale in a local real estate agent's office. The prices were a revelation to me. Properties around Owen Sound were much less expensive than those we'd been looking at near Caledon Lake, no doubt because Caledon Lake is about 50 miles from Toronto and Owen Sound is over 100 miles. Obviously if we wanted a place in the country, we would have to accept a longer drive. We loved living in downtown Toronto, but our souls needed time in the country to bring balance to our lives.

Looking systematically at available properties around Owen Sound, we soon became discouraged. Either prices were too high or the land was unappealing. Houses that were affordable were graceless and devoid of character. What we were looking for was an old house we could rescue and restore.

Finally, at the end of a long Saturday in October during which our agent had shown us one unsuitable property after another, and just when we were almost ready to give up, we found what we thought we wanted. It was a derelict two-story red brick farmhouse with one wall about to crumble, a barn verging on total collapse, and 75 acres of beautiful rolling farmland. It was situated near Massey, a charming village complete with a scenic mill pond. With boundless confidence in our ability to renovate a decomposing house (after all, we had had two years' experience fixing up our Toronto house), and egged on by a price we could actually afford, we decided to buy the property. But because we wanted to go straight back to Toronto, the agent agreed to prepare the offer to purchase back in Owen Sound and mail it to us in Toronto. Our mission was accomplished.

Two days later, when the offer to purchase had not even had time to arrive in the mail, the phone rang while we were having dinner. To our surprise it was a classmate from university days who was now a surgeon in Owen Sound. He was at a dinner party in Toronto and had been told we were looking for property in the Owen Sound area. "Thought you might be interested," he said, "a local minister, Fred Miller, has an old stone house near Owen Sound and wants to sell it. You might give him a call." I thanked him politely as I wrote down the telephone number. In fact, the last thing Andrew and I wanted to do was reconsider our decision to buy the house in Massey.

Nevertheless I phoned Fred Miller right away. We arranged that the very next morning my mother and I would drive up to Owen Sound to look at his stone house. We met him on the highway just south of Owen Sound. I parked the car and we got into Fred's. Away we went.

Fred drove us a short distance south, then east on the Derry Line. The landscape, unlike the rolling, lush countryside on the approach to "our" red brick house, was godforsakenly flat and vacant, neglected pasture alternating with scrubby bush. Not at all promising.

Suddenly, another turn to the south and the landscape improved dramatically. Mature woodland lay to the left. We passed an old, stone, one-roomed schoolhouse and then the road led us to the top of a large hill. The view was breathtaking. The stone house far below was a dream come true.

Fred Miller had known exactly how to beguile us. What a wonderful way he had chosen to introduce us to the house and the Queen's Valley.

NOW IT WAS TIME for closer inspection. We drove down the long lane skirting the foot of the hill, past a majestic but doomed elm tree and around the barn. Finally, there was the house right in front of us.

It sat "firm on its foundations" on a rise of land, the sunlight burnishing the blue, black, brown and rose highlights of the granite blocks. "1876" was clearly carved on the keystone under the gable. A venerable apple tree stood slantingly on guard outside the kitchen door, looking perilously close to the end of its lifespan, but 30 years later it still thrives.

Inside the house, windows—six feet high with painted, panelled reveals—pierced the two-and-a-half foot thick stone walls. Sunlight poured into the largely vacant rooms. Coal oil lamps, wood-burning stoves and a kitchen pump indicated that there were no modern conveniences, although intriguingly, there was a telephone.

Then Fred took us to inspect the rest of the property. The lane led first to the creek north of the house and then swung sharply east up the hill behind the house. Our climb led us past cherry trees, a huge maple and an ancient wide-spreading silvery beech, all on our left. Once again we paused on the brow of a hill and gazed at the fields sloping down to the broad sweep of the Queen's Valley. A short walk down the hill led us to a small ravine carved out by the creek as it headed southeast to join the Bighead River. Here, the creek left the fields behind, plunging into a mature woodlot last harvested in the mid-forties. Ash, hemlock, ironwood, maple, beech and cedar were all to be seen, providing cover for foxes, raccoons, skunks, porcupines, grouse, deer and more recently, coyotes. The creek splashed onward, bouncing over rocky outcroppings, drops sparkling in the sun. It was unbelievably beautiful.

By this time I was bursting with impatience to tell Andrew where serendipity had led us. Fred agreed we could re-visit the farm on our own the very next weekend and told me where to find the hidden key. Once back to the car, my mother and I headed straight for Toronto. I have no memory at all of what I told Andrew or how he responded, but the following weekend, I did exactly what Fred had done. We stopped the car at the top of the hill. Andrew got out and looked at the Queen's Valley in the distance and the stone house just below. He was smitten.

Andrew never questioned my impetuous decision to buy the house, but that was no surprise. Andrew and I had met within weeks of starting university in 1953. We would get married and have our first child, Nickie, before we even left medical school—unusually impetuous for the times.

In the 60s, after we both finished medical school, Andrew went on to get a Ph.D. at the University of Toronto. As for me, I worked full-time for two years, switching to part-time after our second child, Nigel, was born. Then, as part of Andrew's post-doctoral program, we spent three years away from Canada—two years in North Carolina and one year in France. When we returned to Toronto from Paris in 1968, we bought our first house—where we still live. It had been built in 1906 and remained in its original (rather awful) state—dark wood everywhere, a tin ceiling complete with a hole for a stove-pipe in the kitchen, tiny rooms, antiquated plumbing, leaky windows and unappealing wallpaper. Fixing this house was good practice for renovating our Sydenham house. Having done so much together, Andrew and I are now very good at knowing what to expect of each other. We truly have lived "happily ever after."

***

To proceed with the purchase, we unwisely engaged a Toronto lawyer. He drew up an offer to purchase which required that the vendor guarantee that the well would never run dry—a foolish requirement given that in the natural order of things, droughts do occur and dug wells do sometimes run dry. But we have always been prone to accept the advice of experts, so we sent the offer to Fred. When the offer was promptly rejected, we were horrified. Convinced we would lose the farm and that someone else would snap it up, we phoned Fred right away and said we didn't care about the guarantee, we wanted the farm. Fred suggested we consult an Owen Sound lawyer which is exactly what we did. We didn't even consider bargaining. With a mortgage from my uncle, the farm was ours! The closing date was December 15, 1970. We were beside ourselves with excitement.

Always practical, Andrew and I wanted to buy some of the house contents from the Millers. We needed the kitchen wood-stove, the Quebec heater in the living room and the hulking, massive Furnola which would overheat our main floor bedroom and warm the upstairs bedrooms through the stovepipes. Then there were about a dozen turquoise-painted "deal" chairs (i.e., chairs made of wood that was cheap and plentiful), a table, an orange-painted oak side-board, bed springs, a propane refrigerator, some old mattresses and pillows, an iron and brass bedstead, a couple of undistinguished chests of drawers, a picnic bench and some coal-oil lamps. We bought them all and many of these articles are still in use, although we eventually sold the propane refrigerator and bought new mattresses.

We planned to take occupancy on December 26 (allowing us to have a proper Christmas with grandparents in Toronto), and thus were concerned that snow might be a problem. Deep snow would hinder bringing in a Coleman stove, food, china, cutlery, saucepans and sleeping bags. The solution was to bring these necessities to the house in late October or early November when the lane would still be free of snow. This we did although we were flouting legal advice. We must not, we were told, put anything in the house until after the closing date—because if we did, the vendor could claim possession. We chose to trust Fred Miller and his wife Ethel. Twenty-eight years later, Fred Miller would officiate at our son's wedding in the garden behind the house.

⁂

MY MOTHER, Oma to friends and family alike, was with us from the very beginning of this wonderful part of our lives. For over two decades she came as frequently as possible to the farm. She always worked with a real sense of joy—helping Nickie, Nigel and me clear the fields of hundreds of hawthorns, planting trees, cleaning out the barn, stripping paint off furniture, weeding in the garden, or, in her last years, polishing brass and copper, mending, washing dishes and dusting furniture. When that was all done, Oma would embroider. In the few months prior to her death in February, 1995, when, despite the obstinate determination she had displayed all her life she was too weak to go "gallivanting," she kept saying how much she wanted to go once more to the farm.

Our invincible Oma in the winter bush.

At age 15, in 1919, when our stone house was only 44 years old, my mother had emigrated from the Channel Islands to Canada with her parents and siblings. In my childhood, she told me endless stories of her life in Guernsey, and of the Georgian stone house in which she had lived, "The Hougues Magues" (pronounced "Hoog Mahg") in the parish of St. Sampson. Over the years she retold these stories many times, first to her granddaughter and grandson, and even later to her great-grandchildren.

We found out that Hougues Magues means "Margaret's stony land." To Oma's great delight we named our house "The Hougues Magues." Made of stone, surrounded by fields which every spring yield evermore stones—fields defined by fence-rows of stones laboriously gathered by previous generations of farmers—our Sydenham house, with its new-but-old name, ties us to precious memories.

Chapter 2

The First Year

W I N T E R

*There is a degree of spirit and vigour infused into ones blood
by the purity of the air that is quite exhilarating.*

Catharine Parr Trail writing of winter in Ontario in a letter, March 14, 1834.

IN MY MEMORY, every weekend of that first winter the sun always shone, the sky was always brilliant blue, the fences were always completely buried by snowdrifts, and triangles of fluffy white snow clung to the bottom corners of the window panes, echoing clichéd images of Christmas.

Every Friday evening the four of us would arrive from Toronto, long after darkness had fallen. We parked on the road at the foot of the hill below our lane. This was not as easy as it sounds. Now it is hard to believe that on the hillcrest there used to be snow banks twelve and fifteen feet high, halfway up the telephone poles. Near our lane, the banks were four feet high and Andrew would have to shovel out a space for the car so that it would obstruct neither traffic, nor the snowplow. (Predictably, Andrew usually had to dig the car out when we were ready to leave.) Once the car was looked after, we'd put on our skis, fingers fumbling in the cold (the temperature was often -25°C), sling on our loaded knapsacks, and head down the lane through the fresh snow towards the house.

Snowdrifts could abruptly double the depth of the snow, quite indiscernible in the dark. Down I'd go. Getting up out of deep snow while encumbered with a large knapsack is difficult on skis. Andrew, who even with the heaviest knapsack, manoeuvres on skis as easily as others do in shoes, was always quick to heave me up. Before long, we came to know where drifts tended to form and our tumbles became less frequent. However, there was always something for Andrew to attend to—problems with the ski harnesses, or articles which had fallen and been left behind, or an overturned toboggan that needed righting. Toboggans proved more of a nuisance than a help. We soon stopped using our toboggan.

If the moon was full, its cold light would be bright enough to cast a shadow. On clear nights, even without a moon, the sky demanded attention, enveloping our being in a way that is never experienced in an urban setting. The universe seemed to proclaim loudly "I am here." The stars and the planets sparkled with breathtaking brilliance that still holds us spellbound after three decades. Regardless of season, the first thing we do after the long drive from Toronto is look at the night sky.

When we arrived at the house there were always ritual tasks to perform: shovelling snow so we could open the kitchen door; lighting coal oil lamps; starting fires in all available stoves; unpacking food and supplies; and finally, crawling into very cold beds. The wood stoves always burned out by early morning. The invading cold would creep into our sleeping bags, awakening us early enough that the sun's tangential rays were still magically transforming our snow-covered fields to a shimmering pink.

❧

THE VERY FIRST NIGHT we stayed at the Hougues Magues, we had company—three couples with six children, making a total of eight adults and eight children to bed, feed and keep warm.

**Andrew and the house in 1971.
Note cedar rail fence and old apple tree near house.**

Two stoves had been put in working order—the wood-stove in the kitchen, and a Quebec heater in what was destined to be our first living room. In these two rooms all 16 of us would have to sleep—the children in the kitchen and the adults in the living room. At bedtime, we set up wall-to-wall mattresses—old, lumpy, blue-ticking mattresses—in both rooms. Come morning, the bedding was stowed in the unused rooms. An out-door privy was available some distance from the house. And we managed as well as could be expected under the circumstances. After two nights, one couple unashamedly retreated to the luxurious home of an Owen Sound friend—the surgeon who had phoned to tell us about the minister who wanted to sell his farm. We all had fun, taking satisfaction in being so Canadianly resourceful, and coping with such primitive conditions in full winter. But we were soon reminded that accidents are always waiting to happen.

One morning the children were outside playing in the deep snow, making tunnels and igloos and enormous snowmen. The men were bringing in firewood they had sawn and split. The women were in the kitchen cleaning up from breakfast—an extended task because the dishwater had to be heated on our wood-stove. Through the back window, I could see Nigel and a friend happily playing in the snow. Suddenly our young guest, the same young boy who had camped with us that summer, dropped out of sight. Instantly I knew what had happened. Right behind the house was the well, about 14 feet deep. In the fall we had noticed it was covered with a garbage can lid. The lid had not been on our list of things to attend to, especially because by December it was covered with snow. Leaping into a snowdrift, Cam had dislodged the lid and plunged into the well. Fearing the worst, I ran outside and around the corner of the house. I was astonished at what had happened. There was no screaming. Everything was under control. Nigel, not yet eight, had seized his friend's arm, hanging on until others came to help. Cam didn't even get his toes wet. But it was very frightening for everyone.

❧

WINTER WAS SERIOUS BUSINESS, as we soon learned. It was all very well for us to contemplate so very naively "going back to nature" and living without modern conveniences such as plumbing and electricity. However, the reality was that we had to drive three hours in the dark on Friday evenings after a full day's work, often on treacherous highways. Then, wearing our heavy knapsacks, we had to ski half a kilometre to reach a totally unheated house when the outside temperature was cruelly cold. Andrew spent hours every weekend chopping and carting firewood, feeding stoves and disposing of ashes. Our tired eyes could not stay open after 9:00 p.m. because coal oil lamps provided such inadequate light for reading. To enjoy 36 hours at the farm, we paid a high price: six hours travelling time, at least 14 hours lost sleeping, and another ten used to tend the stoves. We wanted more disposable time and so we conceded that modern conveniences—electricity, plumbing and a furnace—would be acceptable.

Modern conveniences are wonderful, but like all technology, they make the user vulnerable, particularly on a farm. If the power, or as we say in Canada, "the Hydro," goes off—which it can for hours at a time in the winter—the furnace stops, the electric stove does not work, and taps cannot be turned on or toilets flushed because the water pump won't function. (To this day we have signs in the bathroom warning visitors not to flush or turn on the taps when the power goes off.) The necessary backups are fireplaces for heat, coal oil lamps for light and a bucket for drawing water directly from the well. Ultimately we would install a propane stove and a propane fireplace, guaranteeing us hot food and a warm room during the longest power outage on the coldest winter day.

But risks still remained—highways made dangerous by whiteouts, ice and stupid drivers. And on the land, always the possibility of getting lost in swirling snow, or becoming hypothermic and falling gently into lethal sleep.

In Canada, winter should not be taken lightly.

❦

IN SPITE OF SNOW, moon and stars, the night was often blackly dark in the winter. During our first winter, the night silence assaulted ears accustomed to the sounds of a lively city. The blackness was relieved only by very occasional house lights in the Queen's Valley and those specks of light seemed very far away. The silence and the sense of isolation we experienced standing at the roadside putting on our skis, thrilled us, but was sometimes unsettling for guests.

Thirty years later, far more lights intrude on the night. Many houses have been built in the valley and beside them bright lights have been installed on tall poles for security reasons. Much more traffic is on the roads, and the northwest skies glow with the light cast by the ever-spreading city of Owen Sound. In another fifty years, will our farm be part of suburban Owen Sound? I'm glad I will never know.

SUMMER

Oh! What a difference since the Hydro came
Cosy little corners don't look just the same
Ev'rywhere a light, now is shining bright
Oh! Oh! Oh! Can't tell day from night.....

Music and Words by Claud Graves, 1912.

THERE WERE SO MANY things we now knew we wanted to do—both inside and out—that priorities were necessary. Hydro (short for hydroelectric power) was the first on the list, because without it nothing would work—not even the plumbing which, of course, required an electric pump. To bring electricity to the house meant we had to run a line in from the road, and to do that we had to buy and install Hydro poles for the power lines. We were wisely extravagant when we chose to bury the lines as they approached the house, leaving the exterior free of unsightly above-ground wires.

But even before electricity, we needed a concrete floor in the basement under the kitchen. No contractor would install a water heater or furnace on a dirt floor, especially a floor that became a sea of mud in the spring. So one of Andrew's first tasks was to arrange for a cement truck to come and pour cement into the basement under the kitchen. He still has vivid memories of how hot it was and how hard the work after the cement had been poured. The cement had to be spread evenly over the entire floor. Then, obeying the instructions of our neighbour, Norm McKibbon (a self-described "builder") Andrew had to keep on smoothing the wet surface intermittently for the next 12 hours.

That first summer at the Hougues Magues, Andrew, already an experienced jack-of-all-trades, functioned as apprentice for his entire holiday. An excellent chef, a skilled water colourist and a musician who plays flute and piano, he readily tackled any project that needed doing at the Hougues Magues. Andrew's energy seemed endless as he

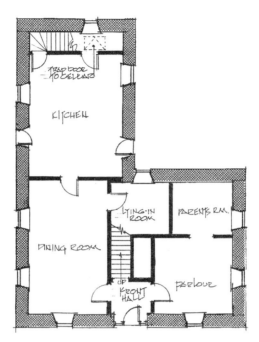

1st Floor

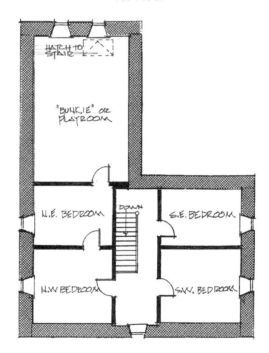

2nd Floor

1970 House layout.
Drawn by George Yost.

completed one task after another—often on the same day. All this, combined with his kind and gentle character explains why Oma endlessly praised her "favourite" (and only) son-in-law.

First, he helped the electrician. It was easy to select the sites for electric switches and outlets, but fishing the electric wires through the non-existent spaces between the stone walls and the wood laths was both frustrating and time-consuming. However, nothing equalled the misery and unpleasantness of slithering on one's belly in the crawl space under the main house, armed with flashlight and assorted tools. Spiderwebs, snakes and groundhogs waited to torment intruders whose only wish was to install the wiring under the main floor as quickly as possible and then to escape from this dark underworld. This is a part of the house I never visit. Unfortunately, it's a rare year that doesn't have Andrew returning to these nether regions for yet another necessary task—installing insulation or new wiring or propane lines. It never ends.

It was 1945 before the farm next door installed Hydro and ours was without electricity until 1971. So we found it quite remarkable that telephones had been installed in the Bognor area by 1911. Even more remarkable to us was that the underground phone line we were using in 1971—all 1100 feet of it extending from road to house—had also been installed in 1911. Local residents had managed very well without electricity, but communication was clearly important to them.

When Bell refused to provide telephone service at the beginning of the 20th century, the Bognor community took up the challenge. Perhaps they were influenced by an advertisement in the *Farmer's Advocate*, May 11, 1911, out of London, Ontario.

"Get your neighbours together and organize an independent telephone service. Buy the telephones and material outright. Make your own rates. Pocket the dividends."

The Bognor Telephone Company was established the same year, later becoming the Sydenham Union Telephone Company. That private phone company with its thirty lines was eventually taken over by Bell Telephone in 1965. Installing a phone was one thing we did not have to worry about.

But we did need to hire a plumber to install bathroom and kitchen plumbing and a furnace. Andrew switched hats and became a plumber's apprentice. Plumbing was basic: a sink in the kitchen, a three-piece bathroom off the main floor master bedroom, and a four-piece bathroom on the second floor for the children and visitors. As for the furnace, the obvious choice was oil and forced air. But that required a chimney. We couldn't afford to face a chimney with stone veneer to match the external walls, and we did not want an ugly concrete-block chimney to deface our beautiful house. The solution was to construct the chimney inside the house, ascending the southeast corner from basement to kitchen, thence into the second-floor playroom and finally through the roof.

This immediately led to more challenges for Andrew. As the chimney rose through the house, it left behind damaged floors and ceilings. The chimney needed to be enclosed. In the kitchen, Andrew surrounded it with a cupboard. Even though the cupboard was largely occupied by the chimney itself, the remaining space was useful for brooms and dustpans. It also became a playground for mice. In the playroom upstairs, Andrew encased the chimney with barn-wood panelling. Eventually, he would deconstruct the entire chimney. Fortunately we did not know that in 1971.

***

THAT FIRST SUMMER there were so many things to do. Leaks needed repairing. The transom over the front door let in rain. The old chimneys allowed rain to enter the upstairs bedrooms, and birds too. Unsightly old stovepipes traversing the bedrooms had to be removed for fear that years of accumulated soot would ignite if they were re-used. Wallpaper, loosened by excessive moisture, dangled into the stairwell making the house feel derelict. It was an enormous job but I found it immensely satisfying to get the house cleaned up. Being tidy (even when guests are not expected) allows me to be efficient—but not surprisingly it draws comment. My children call me "Tidy-Up-Baines."

We wanted to make the Hougues Magues feel cozy and comfortable as quickly as possible. The challenge was to do it without spending money. A pseudo-Scandinavian coffee table with an inlaid veneer chessboard which Andrew and I had made before we were married, was useful in the living room. A bedraggled couch left behind by the previous owners of our Toronto home arrived at the farm tied on the top of our station wagon. We hung simply framed, inexpensive hunting prints on the walls (they are with us still) and arranged knick-knacks on windowsills. The Hougues Magues soon felt like home.

Nigel, an adventurous child, and Nickie, happy and helpful by nature, never ran out of things to do at the farm. Both delighted in exploring the barn. It was filled with wonderful treasures: rusty horseshoes, a red-painted and stencil-decorated wooden winnower, and even old, salvageable furniture. With endless patience they went to the sun-burned fields and picked wild strawberries, sweet beyond description. We argued about which way was the best (and only) way to eat them. Would it be fresh berries for dessert, or cooked berries for jam? The children wanted jam and I thought fresh was better. Or was it the other way around? It doesn't matter. We did both.

Nigel and Nickie tell me they loved drinking from the large aluminum dipper that hung by its long handle on the kitchen pump, always on duty for thirsty people. (When told this, I felt slightly guilty. Long ago I threw it out because of its metallic taste.) They played tetherball noisily, often collapsing with laughter. They picked green beans from our first vegetable garden and helped me freeze them. They foraged on the banks of the creek which previous residents had used as a garbage dump, retrieving a splendid collection of old glass bottles and pieces of farm equipment. Far to the rear of the property in one of the wide-spreading ancient beeches, Nigel built a large tree house with the help of friends and his father—the wood all hauled laboriously from the barn. Then, to amuse them, there was the pony, Prince, who lived next door. When mounted, Prince would never budge an inch.

Even in the house, adventures happened. One stormy day in the brief period between installation of electricity and plumbing, Nickie and I were on our hands and knees in what was still the northeast bedroom. We were painting the dismantled iron and brass bedstead we had bought from the Millers, paying no attention to the lightning and thunder and rain outside—unlike our neighbours who regardless of the hour would always be outside the moment lightning flashed to check if their barns had been struck. To our amazement, a fireball suddenly came through the open window, crossed the room above our heads and hit an electric switchplate where it caused a flash of light and blew a fuse. Since then I've read that there is controversy as to whether such fireball phenomena actually occur. Andrew's mother observed one at the Caledon Lake cottage, and I know we saw one.

It was Nigel who explored the most interesting site on the farm. Close to the creek and north of the original barn were the remnants of an orchard and the almost hidden foundation of a long-vanished cabin where the first settlers lived before they built our stone house in 1876. Among fragments of charred wood, Nigel found a U.S. half-dime which he claims was dated 1853. Could it have been linked to young John Muir, the pacifist and conservationist who later would found Yosemite Park and the Sierra Club? In 1849 at age 11, this young Scot had emigrated to the U.S. with his family. To avoid involvement in the Civil War, he and his brother Dan spent several years in the Bighead Valley during the mid-1860s working at the Trout's sawmill in Meaford making rakes and brooms. It was while living there that Muir began to be concerned about the pillaging of the land, horrified by the wasteful burning of acres of forest.

Life, even without modern conveniences, was easier for us in the summer of 1971, much easier than it would have been for those living on our farm a hundred years earlier. At the end of the day when we were all hot and dirty and tired, we'd climb into the car and drive south for half a concession. We'd park by the bridge over the Bighead River and scramble down the muddy bank. While cattle watched us in their usual, ridiculously solemn fashion, we would swim happily in the cool and refreshing water. That river was a godsend before our plumbing became functional.

WE WANTED TO improve the land as well as restore the house right from the beginning. But looking after the land was going to require long-term vision and a lot of work. The work would proceed incrementally.

When we bought the farm, the original barn was still standing. Rubble in an adjacent field was all that remained of a previous structure, probably an addition to the original barn. Now the debris was strewn over a large area. Stones, rotting timbers, siding and bits of metal cluttered the field and prevented cultivation, so we cleaned it up. The barn however was showing ominous signs of impending collapse. The traditional Ontario barn stands on stone foundations and survives Canadian winters only if animals reside within. The animals generate sufficient heat to prevent the foundation from freezing and cracking. Our barn had not sheltered animals for many years. Like so many Ontario barns, its days were numbered. Within a few years we would dismantle, relocate and rebuild our barn.

Our pasture was neglected. The prime characteristic of neglected pasture—infestation with hawthorns—was all too well revealed in our fields. Hawthorns are at one and the same time, cruel, indestructible, beautiful, useful and devilish. Cruel—because they bear long thorns which penetrate thick work gloves, rubber boots and leather soles and then release a painful toxin at the puncture site. Indestructible—because after being cut to the ground, they defiantly grow back. Beautiful—especially when they display their white blossoms in spring and their vibrantly iridescent orange-red berries in the late afternoon autumnal sun. Useful—because they yield haws (berries) which provide food for wildlife. Devilish—because when grazing cattle eat the haws, new plants spring up wherever cow-pats are dropped.

We had thousands of hawthorns to eradicate if we were to improve our land. Oma, Nickie, Nigel and I traversed the fields, back and forth, armed with long-handled clippers, cutting them close to the ground. This was not always easy because hawthorn stems can be 2 or more inches thick. Then I would cautiously coat the cut surface with Roundup. We stopped counting at 1400! Next we ploughed the fields, which uprooted the very young hawthorns and exposed their roots to air and sun. Those that weren't killed would later be mercilessly severed when the hay was cut.

But there was more to do. All the fence-rows were marked by stately elm trees, many up to three feet in diameter. In 1971, even city dwellers knew about Dutch elm disease which was destroying Ontario's signature tree. Many of the elm trees on our farm were still alive, but all were marked by this fungal disease. It was spread from tree to tree by a bark beetle, thought to have arrived in the U.S. in the 1930s in a shipment from Holland. The most spectacular of all our elms was the one by the lane near the barn. The only sign of disease in 1971 was a small patch of dead leaves in the crown; within four years the tree would be dead. Disposing of the dead elms would keep us busy over many autumns.

We also dreamed about having a pond during that first summer. If swimming in the muddy Bighead River was so refreshing, how much better it would be to swim in our own pond! We were very lucky. The creek, which crossed our fields on its course to the Bighead River, continued through a flat, marshy area, and then entered our bush, plunging downward through a small ravine. All we had to do

Always cheerful, Oma works with grandson Nigel.

was build a dam and widen the ravine and we would have a beautiful pond. But not the first summer.

Over time we developed a management plan that divided our 150 acres into three functional areas. First there were the 25 acres of the original woodlot which needed protection from grazing cattle. Then there were about 60 acres, mainly flat, which would be reasonably good for agricultural purposes once we had improved the pasture and built adequate fences. Left were 65 mainly hilly acres which we were advised to reforest. Our goals and tasks were established.

We have since come to completely agree with an anonymous Irish poet who wrote more than a thousand years ago:

Tis a merry thing to see
At our tasks how glad are we!

quoted in *How the Irish Saved Civilization* (Thomas Cahill, Doubleday, 1995).

MOST CHANGES on the farm evolved slowly. Gradually the fences took shape. Gradually the hawthorns became less numerous. Imperceptibly, the trees we planted, initially hidden by tall grasses and weeds, grew taller. Dozens of dead elms were felled and burned without the landscape appearing to change. And slowly, the fields changed shape.

In contrast, when the Hydro came, the change was radical and instantaneous. To paraphrase the old Ontario song, never since have things been the same.

In the flickering light of coal oil lamps, the rooms lost definition, seemed mysteriously large, the walls amorphous in the shadows, the corners dark. In the brightness of electric lights, the rooms seemed to shrink, all corners illuminated. There were no secrets. Without electricity, the house emanated a heavy silence. With electricity, the background sounds of the refrigerator defrosting, the furnace blowing hot air and the plumbing gurgling intermittently, were constant evidence of how busy a wired house is. The personality of the house is now very different.

I sometimes wonder what the family who built our house would have thought could they have heard our record player suffusing their home with the sounds of soloists, choirs and orchestras from all over the world performing everything from jazz to Handel's *Messiah* and Wagner's *Ring Cycle*. (They could not be amazed about television because there has never been a television set at the Hougues Magues.) Of course, what Angus and Margaret McArthur, the first settlers on our land, would think is impossible to know. But I suspect Angus would have been most interested in Andrew's chainsaw and Margaret, with so many children, might have yearned for my washing machine and dryer.

Chapter 3

First Neighbours

*By the bye, the Dunsfords laid in three hundredweight of butter
for their winter supply, and consumed fifty pounds in three weeks.
You see we gossip of each others' affairs here as elsewhere.*

Anne Langton in a letter, January 17, 1839.

B Y THE END of the summer of 1971 we were beginning to make
friends with some of our neighbours. To our immediate south,
on the farm where they had been born, lived Eddy and Mary
Morrison, an elderly brother and sister, he a bachelor and she a widow.
There have always been a lot of Morrisons around the village of
Bognor. They weren't all related which is why, a long time ago, Mary
Morrison could marry Speely Morrison—the grandson of Angus and
Margaret McArthur who had built our house in 1876. Speely's parents, Sarah McArthur and Dan Morrison, bought our farm in 1900 so
Mary and Speely would have known each other as youngsters, living
as they did on adjacent farms. However, long before Speely was killed
in a car crash, Mary had left him and returned to her childhood home
to live with her brother Eddy, who would take over his family farm in
1945. By 1967, the year of Canada's centennial, theirs would be designated a Century Farm because it was owned and operated by the
third generation of the original family.

Although their two-storied, red brick house was spacious, Eddy and Mary's existence was confined mainly to the kitchen, cool in the summer and cozy in the winter, sleeping in two tiny adjacent rooms. Mary seemed to spend most of her time eating chocolate bars (forbidden food because she had diabetes) and looking with a sharp eye out her kitchen windows.

From the moment we arrived, Mary gave us her undivided attention. "Yass," she'd say with a beaming smile, "Andrew is a re-ee-uul farmer." The fact that Andrew worked hard, got filthy and sweated like a navvy was sufficient evidence for her. Eddy, shyly quiet, carefully tended his land, never allowing hawthorns or thistles to take over. And his fences were always kept in good repair.

Much later we would realize how hard the winter was on these two souls. Their lane was much shorter than ours, but it was a long, uphill grade to the road. Once the snow fell, Eddy parked the car near the road. Mary, unable to walk that distance, spent the entire winter in the kitchen.

Across the road from us lived Norm and Frieda McKibbon. When Norm was still going to school, his parents had briefly lived in our house. Later, when he and Frieda were married in 1943, they made their first home there. Norm told us how he had chiselled off the ceiling rosettes in the main rooms on the first floor to make them more pleasingly "modern" and how he'd been the one who had closed off the alcove in what was originally the front parlour. Unwittingly he had trapped a chair in the space. We would rescue it very soon after our arrival. (Later we found the chair and the Miller's orange sideboard illustrated in a turn-of-the-century Eaton's Catalogue.)

Norm also told us that when he was still living at home with his parents, the basement under the kitchen would flood with the spring runoff. One year the water was so high it almost reached the kitchen floor. That was the year Norm saw rats swimming in the water! We never did see any live rats. Frieda claimed that was because her cat Orange had killed them all, but when we removed the kitchen wall

Norm "The Builder."

which enclosed the stairs going up to the playroom, we found evidence of previous rat habitation. On top of one of the two door frames we were removing, we found a nest made of straw and bits of fabric and paper. In the nest was an old-fashioned silver-plated teaspoon. Only a rat could have put it there.

According to Norm, the early settlers regarded our region as "good growing land." For them, the abundance of stones indicated the soil would be rich in minerals. The settlers were right. It was good growing land, but only as long as agriculture was not mechanized. Horses easily went up and down the hills and around the huge boulders dotting the fields. But tractors were another story. When tractors became the norm in Sydenham Township, our property ceased to have value as a farm. It became a "starter farm." Newlyweds would buy or rent it, stay for a year or two, save enough for a down payment on a better farm, and then move on.

Norm and Frieda stayed longer, from 1943 until 1951 when they sold the stone house and some of their land. They moved just across the road to a slightly newer red-brick house, a large barn and 100 acres of gently rolling agricultural land. But Norm held onto a right-of-way through our original 75 acres to a land-locked 75-acre parcel of land which he kept for grazing his "cattle beasts" (as beef cattle are called around Bognor). Shortly after we got to know them, the McKibbons agreed to sell us the right-of-way and the land. As well, Norm was prepared to rent our entire property for grazing. This suited us very well. Our holding was legitimized as a farm if a farmer rented it, making us eligible for government grants such as the ones for removing dead elms and fence building. As a member and subsequent director of the Ontario Forestry Association, I knew that good forest management required keeping livestock out of woodlots. We would have to protect our forest from Norm's cattlebeasts and we couldn't do that unless we built strong fences.

Norm, being both a farmer and a contractor (his truck was emblazoned with "Norm The Builder"), was an endless source of practical advice. He told us which plumbers, roofers and electricians to use, where to buy replacement sash windows and who to call for concrete and gravel. He lent us seeders and tractors. He taught us how to play horseshoes. He told us stories. He called square dances in the community hall. He teased us endlessly. And he was always ready to share his wisdom. "The only person a locked door ever stops is an honest man" was one of his sayings. When Frieda informed him that one of our guests whom they'd met was a "professor at the university," Norm's wise response was "Frieda, yass is yass and no is no, never mind who says it."

⁂

It became an annual ritual for as long as Nickie and Nigel spent their holidays at the farm for the two of them to help Norm with the haying. They learned the meaning of the expression "Let's make

Nickie haying at the McKibbons.

hay while the sun shines." If it rains, cut hay cannot be baled until it has dried out. So after the hay has been cut and stretches in long rows in the field, the big question always is, will it rain before we get it baled?

Under the stunningly blue Sydenham skies, Nickie and Nigel rode on the wagon and stacked the rectangular bales of hay as they emerged from the baler. There were always two teams working—one in the fields where the work was hot and heavy, and another in the barn where sneezing was the order of the day. Nevertheless, the barn workers were lucky. Not only was it cool compared to being in the fields, they could also enjoy a quick game of horseshoes between wagonloads. As for the field hands, when they got thirsty they could always get a drink from the gallon jug of water that Frieda had frozen earlier. The jug, stashed between rocks in a fence row, melted gradually over the course of the day, so everyone could enjoy a cold drink of water. Etiquette required that as the jug passed from one to another, one did not wipe the mouth of the bottle. Nigel, somewhat fastidious, did this once and was severely rebuked.

Nickie remembers one particular day when she stacked an entire wagonload on her own. Mel Morrison, Norm's next door neighbour and by then retired from farming, was helping Norm. Mel hitched the wagon Nickie had so carefully loaded to his tractor and headed off for Norm's barn. Not quite as safety-conscious as he would have been in the past, he headed straight down the hill. The wagon broke loose from the tractor and hurtled downhill arriving at the bottom intact. Nickie was still on top and not one bale had fallen off. Norm looked at Nick and said laconically, "Well, you can stack a good wagon." Then, according to Nickie, he turned to Mel and "gave him hell." Later, other neighbours would insist on paying Nickie at haying time "because she did a man's work." Nigel was paid too, but that was expected because, after all, he was a male.

Both Nickie and Nigel would profit from observing firsthand the unending patience and extraordinary ingenuity farmers exercise as they set about repairing equipment using parts scavenged from whatever is at hand. Has ever a baler operated during the whole haying season without once breaking down?

❦

GOOD FOOD was the reward for anyone who helped with the haying: dinner at noon and supper at the end of the afternoon. Depending on the size of the farm, wives in Sydenham could end up preparing meals for as many as a dozen hungry workers. A typical dinner menu would be hot roast beef (or ham or pork) served with boiled potatoes, vegetables from the garden, homemade pickles and tea biscuits. Always standing in the middle of the table would be a "water jar" of whole green onions. Sometimes another jar would hold celery stalks. There would be tea and water to drink and pies for dessert. Supper was often late and always cold: leftover meat from dinner, homemade coleslaw and potato salad, tomatoes, and cake and fruit.

Elizabeth Gillies (pronounced "Gillis"), fourth generation in the area, remembers with amusement one 15-year-old from Bognor who had come to help with the haying. He took one look at her cold supper, then "fled for home rather than eat salads." He knew his mother, Betty Murdoch would make him a hot meal. The young helper, Bill Murdoch, is the current provincial Member of Parliament for our riding.

Elizabeth also recalls that there was never any "drinking" (that is, of alcoholic beverages) at haying time, but "barn raisings were something else." I suspect "Shwish," a local specialty—namely inexpensive, watered-down alcohol—may have hit the spot for thirsty workers at some barn raisings. Don Emmerson, another neighbour whom we would get to know very well, gave us the recipe. First you buy an oak barrel "for $25.00 from a distiller in Barrie," he explained. "Then add two or three gallons of water to the barrel and shwish the fluid around in the barrel at least once a day for about a month." We have actually tasted it. The "water" is interestingly flavoured with a spiritous essence. But Don doubts that people are making Shwish anymore.

The very first Sydenham recipe I ever requested was the one for Frieda's tea biscuits. Nickie and Nigel had enjoyed them so much when they were haying up at the McKibbons that they wanted me to make them too. Both still make them, and so do I. Tea biscuits are handy if you have unexpected company and want something nice for afternoon tea.

Frieda McKibbon's Tea Biscuits

Sift together 2 cups sifted all-purpose flour with 4 tsp baking powder, 3 tbsp sugar and 1/4 tsp cream of tartar. Place in bowl with 1/2 cup shortening (or butter) and chop with pastry cutter until the texture of coarse meal. Add 3/4 cup milk. Clump dough together with hands in the bowl, and then roll out on floured board. Cut into 3/4 inch thick rounds using the rim of a glass tumbler. Place rounds on greased cookie sheet. Prick surface with fork. Brush tops with milk or a glaze made of an egg yolk beaten with 1 tsp of cold water. Bake at 450°F for 10 minutes until golden brown and serve immediately.

These are good with butter alone, or with jam, or even better with whipped cream and strawberry jam. They must be served hot and do not keep well.

Coleslaw was also served during haying season. We liked it whenever we were having hotdogs or hamburgers for lunch. Nowadays it is very tempting to buy ready-made coleslaw, but home-made is much better!

Hougues Magues Coleslaw

Shred finely 1/2 medium-sized green cabbage and place in a large bowl. Grate 2 medium-sized carrots and add to cabbage. Add 1/4 cup or more raisins. In a small saucepan, beat 1 egg with 1 tbsp sugar, 1 tsp salt, 1 tsp dry mustard and 1/2 tsp ground pepper. Add 3 tbsp white vinegar and 1 tbsp soft butter. Cook, stirring over a low heat until it thickens. If lumps form, remove from heat and beat until smooth. When thickened, add 2 tbsp milk or cream and mix well. Pour over cabbage mixture and mix thoroughly. Let dressed salad stand at least one hour in refrigerator before serving.

Chapter 4

How the Land Began

"They (aboriginal land claims) arise, in general terms, from breaches of treaty, breaches of trust, and circumstances such as theft of land and flagrant violation of the fiduciary duties of the Crown."

**James Prentice speaking to the
Canadian Bar Association, April, 2000.**

ROM NEW YORK STATE and the Niagara River to Collingwood, where it forms the Blue Mountain, extending up the Saugeen (now the Bruce) Peninsula and across to Manitoulin Island, and then curving in an arc to end west of Chicago. That is the path of the Niagara Escarpment, an inescapable, craggy presence for us in Grey County where Sydenham Township is located. Pre-dating the glacial age, the Niagara Escarpment is a topographic break in the bedrock produced by differential erosion of harder and softer rock. The escarpment resisted erosion more than the land along its margins, thus its pre-eminence in the landscape. Also dating from pre-glacial times are the Bighead and Beaver Valleys, which were carved out of bedrock. Later, the Wisconsin glacier covered the land and moved back and forth, retreating and advancing. This movement eroded what lay beneath. Soil and rock were mixed together and milled, producing glacial till.

The Niagara Escarpment, proclaimed by UNESCO a World Biosphere Reserve, has given Southern Ontario its highest hills and best downhill skiing—the Blue Mountain and Georgian Peaks. What I mistakenly believed in 1970 to be the "foothills of the Blue Mountains," are actually a promontory of the escarpment separating the Beaver from the Bighead Valleys. The escarpment has given Grey County its spectacular scenery: dramatic cliffs both inland and along the shoreline of the Bruce Peninsula as well as three stunning waterfalls, Inglis Falls, Jones Falls and Indian Falls in the Owen Sound area alone. And then, under the surface of the escarpment, gravel. Gravel to make roads. Gravel to make wealth. How much gravel has, will, or should be mined from the Niagara Escarpment, gives rise to continuing dissension.

Drumlins (Celtic for "little hill") are another reminder of our glacial past. These characteristic glacial droppings were first named "drumlins" in 19th century Ireland. Before then they were called sowbacks or whalebacks. Oval in shape and clustering together in "drumlin fields," drumlins, like sheep, tend to point in the same direction, the line of glacial retreat. As the glacier melted, it left the drumlins behind. Drumlins can be as high as 150 feet, extending for more than a mile, or they can be no more than slight undulations in the land up to two miles in length.

There are over 6000 drumlins in Ontario, distributed in eight main regions. The largest region is circumscribed by a line joining Port Hope to the east, Picton to the west, and Lake Simcoe to the north. Another cluster of drumlin fields, (all pointing north, so that was the way the glacier moved), is located in the Bighead Valley south of Owen Sound and Meaford. These drumlins are described in *The Physiography of Southern Ontario* as "standing up plainly" and measuring 75 to 100 feet in height and anywhere from 1000 feet to half a mile in length. Two drumlins are on our land. One provides our fastest skiing hill. The second is covered by our woodlot. Made as they are of glacial till, they have good soil, but for agricultural purposes, their limitations were, and still are, steep slopes and too many stones.

From "Redman," "Indian" and "Squaw" to "First Nations"—over time, language and attitudes have changed so much in Canada, a change bluntly apparent when you read the histories of Grey County written over the last century. What has not changed is that everyone has always recognized First Nations were here long before Europeans arrived. The first Europeans to visit the area may very well have been Samuel de Champlain and his companions in the early 17th century. By the late 1640s, the Jesuits had published maps showing Lakes Ontario, Huron and Superior, quite accurately placing Manitoulin Island, the Bruce Peninsula, Owen's Sound and both Georgian and Nottawasaga Bays. The earliest visits by Europeans were in search of beaver pelts, so plentiful in the Valley of the Beaver, now known as the Beaver Valley. From that time on, First Nations people endured cruel inter-tribal battles, mortal new diseases, physical dislocation and shabby treatment by government officials. In Grey County and all over Canada, First Nations people who managed to survive (they didn't in Newfoundland) eventually found themselves sequestered in regions which did not allow them to live off the "land and waters" as they had previously. Church-run residential schools and a federal bureau of Indian Affairs rendered too many First Nations people passively dependent and often explicitly deterred educational ambition. Drug and alcohol abuse soared while the fat- and carbohydrate-loaded North American diet has induced a tragic burden of diabetes. A sad legacy.

The story of an "Indian Princess," Nahneebahweequa Sonego (The-Woman-Who-Stands-Straight-and-Tall Black Squirrel), also known as Catherine Sonego, always appears in histories of Grey County. She was born to Ojibwa parents (called Mississauga by Europeans) in 1824 near the Credit River (present-day Mississauga, Ontario) and was educated at the local Methodist Mission school. When her father, who was a chief, decided to return to the Grand River band near Brantford, the child was turned over to the care of her uncle and aunt, Peter and Eliza Jones, so that she could continue her education. Eliza was English and Peter was half Ojibwa, a Mississauga chief whose Indian name was Kahkewaquonaby. Seeking to raise funds for their missionary work and also to petition the British Colonial Office against proposed relocation plans for Indian Bands in Upper Canada, the Jones's took Catherine to England for a year in 1837.

After returning to Canada, Catherine married William Sutton on January 9, 1839 at the Credit River village. He was an English Methodist lay preacher who had been in Canada since 1830. In 1846 the Suttons, along with two other families from the Credit River band, moved to the Owen Sound area. There the Nawash band gave the Suttons 200 acres of land in what is now the Townships of Keppel and Sarawak just north of Owen Sound.

An 1846 map of Upper Canada published by Joseph Bouchette, Surveyor General, clearly indicates that all land north of what is now the city of Owen Sound, including the entire Bruce Peninsula, was an "Indian Reserve." All this land had been assigned to the Ojibwa in an 1836 Surrender Treaty. Yet in 1857, the Suttons' land was parcelled into lots and sold off at public auction. Why did this happen even though Catherine and her husband had cleared 50 acres and built a house, stable and barn on this land?

The story begins with the defeat of the French in North America in 1759 and the British Royal Proclamation of 1763. The Proclamation not only recognized that Indian Nations had a right to their lands, but also provided a mechanism whereby the Crown could negotiate with Indian Nations (not individuals) to acquire land from them. Individual Indians could no longer be duped by unscrupulous land speculators into selling land at unreasonably low prices. A benefit to the Crown was that peaceful relations with the Indian Nations were encouraged. Even more important, it was hoped that the proclamation would encourage Indian Nations to provide the Crown with military support in the event of any conflict, such as the American War of Independence.

Much later, after the War of 1812, such strategic benefits vanished and the inflow of European immigrants accelerated. Europeans regarded any land used solely as a hunting ground to be unproductive and not in fact "settled." This attitude enabled them to rationalize taking over the land from the Indians. Nevertheless it was required that the Crown be an intermediary between the Indians and the settlers. The Crown fulfilled this role by means of treaties such as the 1836 Surrender.

Prior to 1836, the Saugeen territory included a vast tract of land, two million acres, the southern border of which stretched from current-day Arthur west to Lake Huron and north from Arthur to Georgian Bay. During the first half of the 19th century, the government encouraged Indians to migrate to this region from more southern parts of Ontario and the USA, particularly Michigan. Thus by the 1830s, the Saugeen Territory was inhabited by several different Ojibwa tribes including the Potawatomi, Mississauga, Nawash and Saugeen. There were even some Mohawks, the Caughnawaga. The mixture of tribal cultures, combined with conflicts between Methodist and Roman Catholic converts, Christians and non-Christians, and hunters and agriculturalists had negative consequences. Solidarity in the struggle against the Crown and its unceasing demands for more and more land was seriously weakened.

By the mid-1830s, Governor-General Sir Francis Bond Head had decided assimilation would not work and that the Indians in Upper Canada would be vastly better off if they all were removed to Manitoulin Island—then a barren landscape noted for its "big rocks and small stones," harsh weather, poor soil, and inadequate game. In short, a place where communities were unlikely to thrive. Bond Head's initiative was not at all welcomed by the Indians. Indeed it was

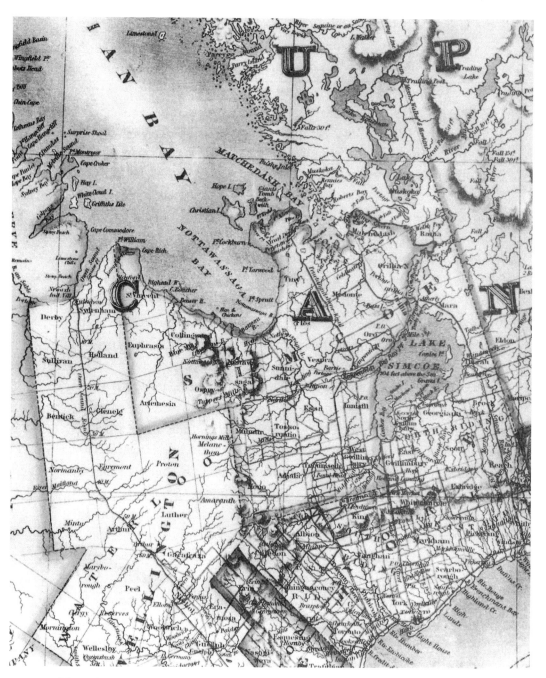

Map of Upper Canada, 1846. Joseph Bouchette and Henry Bayfield. Part of a map of the provinces of Canada...according to the treaties of 1842 & 1846. Engraved by Sherman & Smith, New York. Joseph Bouchette, New York, 1846.

National Archives of Canada, NMC 48910, part 4 of 6 sections.

to petition against this specific initiative that Peter Jones went with his wife and young Catherine Sonego to England in 1837. Responding to their petition, the Colonial Secretary, Lord Glenelg withheld consent for Bond Head's Manitoulin Island plan. Unfortunately, Bond Head had already succeeded in having the 1836 Surrender finalized, bearing the signatures of seven Europeans and five Indians. The treaty read:

> "I now propose to you that you should surrender to
> your Great Father the Sauking (Saugeen) Territory you at
> present occupy, and that you shall repair either to this
> Island (Manitoulin) or to that part of your territory which
> lies on the North of Owen Sound, (this refers to the body
> of water, not the city which was not named until later)
> upon which proper houses shall be built for you, and proper
> assistance to enable you to become civilized and to cultivate
> land, *which your Great Father engages forever to protect for you
> from the encroachments of the whites.*" (italics mine)

(Indian Treaty No. 45 1/2).

The 1836 Surrender relinquished 1.5 million acres of land. Bond Head claimed that the Saugeen Chiefs "cheerfully gave up this great tract of land," in return for the promise that their fishing rights would be protected. (A false promise, as recent litigation demonstrates.) Eighteen years later, in 1854, the Great Father's 1836 assurances to the contrary, all of the Saugeen (Bruce) peninsula was surrendered to the Crown, leaving only five small Indian reserves. Even that was not enough to satisfy the demand for land. In 1857, the Nawash reserve, one of the five established with the 1854 Surrender, the reserve where the Suttons had settled, was itself surrendered. A local Methodist minister, Conrad Vandusen, stated at the time that "the Crown had conducted its negotiations with an unofficial and unrepresentative group of Nawash band members" in clear violation of the spirit of the Royal Proclamation. The Nawash band was forced to abandon cleared land,

Catherine Sutton c. 1860.
With permission from County of Grey–Owen Sound Museum.

homes, barns, schools and church and to re-locate to Cape Croker where the land was poor and conditions harsh. Further Surrenders would be extracted in 1861, 1885 and 1886.

When the Suttons' farm was put up for auction, Mrs. Sutton's offer to purchase her own land for $5.00 per acre for 49 1/2 acres was not challenged even though $5.00 was well under the market price. No one wanted to bid against her. Nevertheless, the government of the day refused to give her the deeds for the land. In spite of petitions to the government and the Legislative Assembly by the Nawash Band and by Methodist missionaries, the government would not change its position. Mrs. Sutton was prohibited from buying her land because she was an Indian. She was also for the rest of her life denied her share of the Nawash band's government annuities because, married to a European, she was not seen to be an Indian. A classic "Catch-22" situation.

Undeterred, Mrs. Sutton toured Canada and the United States to raise funds to enable her to appeal personally to Queen Victoria in

England. On March 4, 1860 she was received by the Queen who promised to investigate the situation further and who recorded the visit in her diary. When Mrs. Sutton returned to Canada, she found that the British government had intervened and her husband had been allowed to purchase the four lots she had previously bid on. Other Nawash Band members were never allowed to buy lots because as Indians, they were minors under the law. Mrs. Sutton died in September, 1865, age 41, in Sarawak Township.

At the end of the 20th century, the rights of First Nations were increasingly being recognized in Canada. Territory wrongfully surrendered is being restored to them and responsibility for governance is being transferred to First Nations leaders. Justice delayed is better than no justice at all.

CAPTAIN WILLIAM OWEN is said to be the first Anglo-Saxon to enter Owen's Sound (a sound is an inlet off a bay), the harbour of the future city of Owen Sound. Charged with surveying the Great Lakes in 1815, he was sailing a vessel which the British had seized from the Americans and renamed the Huron. Captain Owen named the Sound after his brother, an Admiral who was Britain's naval Commander of the Lakes. It would be another thirty-two years until Charles Rankin, a provincial land surveyor, surveyed the area where the town of Sydenham would be built. Named in 1840 after Lord Sydenham, then the Governor General of Canada, this town would become the future city of Owen Sound.

As for Sydenham Township, it was surveyed in 1843, a time when settlers were establishing themselves in Collingwood, Thornbury and Meaford and were gradually moving westward along the shoreline. Many miles to the south, others were settling in Fergus and Arthur and from there, settlers would move northward overland. Their lot was much harder. No roads. Huge trees to fell. Swarms of mice invading their beds. Hordes of biting insects. Starvation. And bitterly cold winters. All would be endured for the sake of a new life.

The same 1846 map of Upper Canada that demarcated the "Indian Reserve" also shows that the Bighead River had already been named. Two stories explain how this came about. One is that earlier surveyors had found a huge skull when camping by the river mouth, hence a "big head." The second claims that the strong river current provided a "big head" to drive the many mills which would later be built on the river.

All the townships in what would be the future County of Grey, including Sydenham, can also be seen on the 1846 map, but it wasn't until 1850 that the Township of Sydenham was actually incorporated. Two years later, at the first meeting of the Provisional Council of Grey (honouring the then Governor General Earl Grey) all these townships were consolidated within the county. Soon after, the Council decided to build the county buildings, the "gaol" and the courthouse, in the town of Sydenham, making it the county seat. A special Act of Parliament, taking effect on January 1, 1857, renamed the town. It was to be called Owen Sound and had a population of 1,945.

Exactly one month later, the Nawash Band was dispossessed of their village and their reserve of 10,000 acres.

MEANWHILE, 12 MILES to the southeast of Owen Sound, Bognor, in the southern part of the Township of Sydenham, was established in 1861 as Sydenham Mills, the land deeded by the Crown to Mr. James Trotter. Expectations were high for this village with its sawmill, flour-mill, and shingle mill all driven by Walter's Creek, a tributary of the Bighead River. The surveyor's map outlined a network of streets including King, Queen, Frank, John and William, street names still common in all Ontario towns and cities. When the Sydenham Mills post office was opened in 1873, it was feared that the village might be confused

Thomson's General Store in Bognor.
Ledgers show the McArthurs and Morrisons shopped here.
Photograph courtesy of the Bognor Women's Institute.

with the town of Sydenham in Frontenac County. The village's second postmaster suggested the new name should be Bognor, the English town where he grew up. Bognor became the official name in 1879.

A Methodist Church was built in 1873, the town hall in 1888 and a small Anglican Church, St. Matthews, in 1901. In its heyday Bognor had two general stores, the first of which was established by James M. Thomson in 1888. There was a butcher who supplied beef to Owen Sound, a weaver, a tombstone maker, a tinsmith, a carriage maker and a supplier of saddles and harnesses. Other facilities included a shoe shop, two blacksmith shops, a cooperage for barrel-making and a basket and broom factory.

No remnant of all this commercial activity remains today. Ontario's rural population began to decline around 1890, accelerating after World War I. Certainly the fire in July 1957, which destroyed the old hall and the commercial buildings was a blow. Later decisions to demolish the two churches and not to restore the pond after the dam washed out, further erased Bognor's brief history. What remains, aside from comfortable homes and pleasant gardens, are a playing field, the Community Hall and the post office.

For a long time, Sydenham Township has partitioned itself. There is North Sydenham, with the villages of Leith, Annan and Balaclava, and South Sydenham where Bognor lies. To this day there is a perceptible if very subtle sense that South Sydenham is on the "wrong side of the tracks." People who have lived in South Sydenham all their lives agree—and say they don't know why. People who have lived in North Sydenham all their lives, from fourth and fifth generation families, cannot understand why anyone would choose to live in South Sydenham, and indeed rarely if ever visit the area.

I think I am beginning to understand how this happened. North Sydenham was settled slightly earlier. It is where the Land Agent, John Telfer chose to settle and land agents were renowned for choosing the best land for themselves and their friends. North Sydenham was where the relatively wealthy were likely to settle, those who could afford to arrive by steamer from Collingwood rather than taking the tough overland route from Arthur. And North Sydenham has probably always had better agricultural land if only because it is less hilly and water could always be drawn from the bay.

In contrast, South Sydenham was settled by the poor Irish, English and Scottish who travelled on foot from the south. Is it a reflection of prosperity or civic commitment that in the *1880 Illustrated Atlas of Grey and Bruce Counties*, among 17 Atlas subscribers listed from Sydenham, not one is from South Sydenham? (Subscribing before publication was rewarded. A short biography of the subscriber was included in the Atlas.)

Later, North Sydenham was where the well-to-do of Owen Sound established their waterfront summer homes. Now some retire there. In Leith, the old church was rescued and restored, and now is the site for important cultural events, weddings and occasional Sunday services. In Bognor, the two churches were torn down and there was no one to speak for architectural conservancy.

Long after memories have faded, a certain mindset persists. But it probably is waning.

Chapter 5

Lives Lived

Pioneers did not produce original works of art because they were creating original human environments; they did not imagine utopias because they were shaping them.

George Woodcock in "An Absence of Utopias," *Can lit* 1969; 42:5.

❧

DICK MURDOCH used to deliver our mail. He's now 86 and still lives in Bognor in the house where he was brought up by his teetotalling grandparents. He remembers bagpipers, three or four at a time, their day's work over, meeting by the pond behind his home to pipe together. He remembers the pipers leading the parade on the 12th of July down Bognor's main street. And he remembers when everyone in the village had a cow. Gardens were fenced and cows were allowed to roam the streets—and so they were free to chase the Orangemen's parade.

When I was a child, everyone knew that on the Twelfth of July traffic stopped on the main streets of towns and cities. It stopped for a parade, always led by a man riding a white horse. That man was a stand-in for King William, irreverently called "King Billy." What I was observing was a pale shadow of the celebrations decades earlier in Ontario when streets would be decorated with orange bunting and Union Jacks. July the Twelfth was always crammed with planned events, including speeches, sporting events and concerts. Today it's difficult to believe that Bognor was once so fervently Orange.

The Orange Order came to Canada in the 1830s with Irish immigrants, Protestants, who felt compelled to defend themselves against Catholicism. Originally, the secret order of Loyal Orange Lodges (LOLs) was a self-help organization for newcomers. However more was involved than self-help. Secret signs, symbols and rituals were integral to LOLs. Oaths were taken pledging fealty to the Monarch (Queen Victoria), the Protestant Succession (no Catholics were wanted on the throne) and the British Empire. The Orangeman's hero was King William, the Prince of Orange, who came from Holland to rule England, and who had in their words "overthrown oppressive bigotry and restored liberty" at the Battle of the Boyne in the seventeenth century. Thenceforth English monarchs would be Protestants.

In Canada the order came to symbolize the polarization between Protestants and Roman Catholics and between English- and French-speaking Canadians. Resentment of Orangemen escalated. They controlled municipal politics until well into the 20th century and it was generally believed they effectively enforced a quota limiting the number of Roman Catholics who could be hired.

The first Orange lodge in Grey County, LOL # 67, was founded by Sydenham residents in 1847 and located in what would become Owen Sound. Before long, because most of the members came from Sydenham Township, the lodge was relocated to the Bognor area where it flourished for more than 100 years, using local homes, churches and schools for its activities.

The *Owen Sound Sun Times* wrote (July 11, 1934):

"All the Order is at the present time it owes to the sturdy men who fearlessly walked on former 'Twelfths' and heroically served the Protestant Cause in all the Provinces."

Ontario has changed radically.

IN 1929 Dick Murdoch, then only 17 years old, was given his grandfather's job. He became the mailman for RR #1, Bognor and delivered the mail to 60 families, six days a week, even on Christmas Day. There were no holidays. "You always knew who was getting married, who should be getting married, and who wasn't," Dick told me, chuckling. The post office was located in Thomson's general store, so it was very easy for people on his route to ask him to bring items from the store: tobacco, liniment, yeast and bread. Most important was the chewing tobacco. If Dick happened to forget, he'd "turn around to get it," adding, "You weren't supposed to deliver groceries; you done it to help people out." He never charged for these services. But in return, Dick knew "if you needed help in any way, you were all right." People would come to his aid. This attitude still prevails in Bognor.

In the early years, Dick had a pair of horses and a cutter. "Horses were better than cars for not skidding down the big hills!" The snow then was much deeper than in recent years and the cold, colder. Up until the late thirties, his winter route bypassed the road going up and down the big hill in front of our house. People called this road the "goat-path" because only goats would want to climb up and down it. To detour the hill, Dick drove across farm fields, around the base of the hill and along part of our lane. Only then would he rejoin the main road. Dick took four hours to do his entire route and when it was really cold, he used to walk behind the cutter rather than ride to keep himself warm. "People wanted their mail every day, even if the roads weren't cleared." His first car deliveries were made in a Model-T Ford. "When you got low on gas, you'd have to back up the steep hill in front of your house," Dick explained, "so that the gas would run into the engine and keep the car running."

But Bognor was not an entirely idyllic village. Fights were frequent, fuelled by "lots of booze" which is somewhat paradoxical because Bognor was officially dry. All the time, Bognor was like the rest of Ontario. In *Greenbank, Country Matters in 19th Century Ontario,* historian W.H. Graham writes: "The vice visible and present beyond all others in 19ᵗʰ century Ontario was the pervasive drunkenness that marks a pioneer society... Whiskey along with its gift of cheer brought domestic misery and economic failure." The temperance movement which had moved from the U.S. into Ontario in the 1840s tried vainly in subsequent decades to persuade parliament to enact effective legislation to control the problem. Finally, as in other small communities, the Bognor town fathers passed bylaws prohibiting hotels so that Bognor could be kept safely dry.

Although Bognor remained dry until recently, it never stopped some people from drinking. The inevitable question arises—where did all the booze come from? Everyone says it was sold at "Starvation Hotel"—no one knows the reason for the name—at a crossroads south of Owen Sound. Fred Miller told another story: he said Dan Morrison ran a still at the back of our farm. Once a week Dan drove his wagon into town to sell his "screech," and he was always so drunk at the end of the day that he slept in the wagon as his horse took him back home.

In fact, Bognor had such a "bad reputation" in the late twenties that Dick's wife Betty told me she was not allowed to visit the village before she got married. Someone else told me that her father used to say "You must be smelling yourselves" if she and her sisters said they were going to Bognor. That expression was new to me. So I was very surprised subsequently to find in Thomas Hardy's *The Return of the Native*, a man scornfully telling his young granddaughter that she had "gone sniffing" when she went to the local village to seek young mixed company. A strange continuity extending over decades and reaching across the Atlantic Ocean.

Living most of the time in Toronto, we frequently noticed other expressions particular to Sydenham. Another neighbour Ruth Carmichael and my mother had parallel habits of speech. Ruth frequently ended sentences with "but anyways." My mother ended sentences with "but however." Again (to my surprise,) that latter phrase is used in George Bernard Shaw's play *Heartbreak House*. Matching the current corporate use of "if you will" as a sentence filler, Sydenham residents use "like they say." And where teenagers are now prone to say "like" several times per sentence as well as between sentence fragments, our neighbours liberally sprinkle the word "really"—only they pronounce it "rilly." However, I can find no parallel in my experience to the Sydenham term "stairsteps" accustomed as I am to using the word "stairs" or "steps" separately, not combined.

Mel Morrison also made us familiar with some Sydenham expressions. Instead of saying "I am going into town," Mel, and others too, said "I do be going to town." I've not heard that expression for a while, but another one Mel used is still heard even when young people are speaking. The words have a special rhythm and are meant to express agreement. Instead of saying simply "Yes" or "You're right," people say "It *is* so" or "It *did* so."

Then there was the expression "storm-stayed" when snow prevented you from leaving your house. Another one was "blue snow," at least that was what we thought we heard. In fact, the expression was "blew snow" as in snow blown by high winds into drifts that blocked lanes and roads. Quite different was a "skiff of snow" which meant a light dusting of snow on the ground.

Mel Morrison and Lloyd Carmichael come to visit.

THE FIRST EUROPEANS to settle on our land were Angus McArthur (1814-1904) and his wife Margaret (1823-1899), both Presbyterian, who emigrated from Scotland. The census records for 1851 reveal that Angus was living on the eleventh concession just east of Rockford. He owned 50 acres and 35 were cleared. Six of his acres yielded 60 bushels of wheat that year, 1 1/2 acres yielded 15 bushels of peas, two acres yielded 50 bushels of oats, 1/2 acre produced 25 bushels of potatoes and 15 acres were woodlot. By 1861 the census recorded that he and Margaret were living in a one-story log cabin on what would become our land. They had at that time seven children, all born in Canada: Mary, John, Thomas, James, Peter, Margaret and Sarah, with Mary the oldest at 15 and Sarah the youngest, one year of age. Sarah would live on the farm until the early 1930s.

The *1865 Gazetteer of Grey County* confirms that Angus and his family were living on our farm although no deed would be registered until much later. How Margaret coped with childbirth and child rearing, winter blizzards, biting insects and summer heat, all in a one-story cabin, is beyond imagination. For eleven more years the McArthurs lived in their log cabin (the site Nigel excavated in 1971), clearing the land, selling logs, sugaring off and growing crops. They must also have gathered granite and limestone rocks—and saved money to pay the stonemasons to build their house. Almost 100 years later, Norm and Frieda McKibbon, like them, would pay for their house by selling logs from the bush at the back of the property. The bush is still there.

The 1871 census notes that Angus and Margaret McArthur had added three more children to their family. Only one of the ten McArthur children was attending school, Peter, age 15. Sadly, the region extending from Orangeville north to Georgian Bay and west to Lake Huron which covers Sydenham Township, was less prosperous compared to other parts of Ontario. Consequently, a much smaller proportion of the population attended school and schools were much more poorly equipped than elsewhere.

Today, one still meets older people, both intelligent and well informed, who are able to sign a cheque but are unable to read or write, all because they had to leave school early to help support their families. As late as the 1960s, children in Sydenham Township still went to one-room schoolhouses for their primary school education. For many years, Betty Murdoch taught in these schools. She showed me a poem she had been given, an anonymous tribute from one of her ex-students.

> As I stood there on the sidewalk
> And thought of days gone by
> I recalled my own first day at school
> And how I'd been so shy.
>
> And how my sister had taken my hand
> As we walked down the 11th line
> Until finally we came to an old stone school
> Known as S.S. No. 9.
>
> A fellow has more than one teacher
> This fact everyone well knows
> And there was one teacher we all came to love
> And her name was Miss Betty Bowes
>
> We remember the "scoldings" you gave us
> To make us "act as we should"
> And looking back over those scoldings now
> We agree they done us good!
>
> Back in those days there weren't any grades
> We never heard tell of the word.
> It was a primer, first and second,
> Then junior and senior third.
>
> That old stone school has played a big part
> In shaping the years still ahead
> And the lessons we learned and impressions we got
> Still haunt us like one from the dead.

BY THE TIME the McArthurs had built their house in 1876, Angus was 62 years old. Four years later, the *1880 Historical Atlas of Counties Grey and Bruce*, records that their son Peter, age 26, is the owner of the farm. However, the first deed registered for the property in 1887 names an older son, James. James sold the farm to Peter in 1891 and their father Angus appears intermittently in the registry records as both a grantor and grantee of mortgages. At the end of 1896, Angus bought the farm from Peter and sold it three months later to a third son, Thomas. Then, in 1899, Thomas McArthur sold it to William McNab who lived across the road.

We wondered why the property changed hands so often until two long-time Bognor families explained that when the "old-timers" were drunk, they would sell their farms "for a dollar or a cow" depending on what they needed at the moment. To this day, some title searches can be a legal nightmare.

The McArthurs' daughter Sarah (1859-1958) married another Bognor resident, Donald (known always as Dan) Morrison (1859-1931). Dan's parents (Neil and Christina Morrison) had emigrated from England. At the time of the 1861 census they were living in a one-story log cabin in Bognor with their one-year old son Dan. In 1900, when forty year-old Dan and his wife Sarah already had several children, they bought "our" farm from William McNab. Whatever the needs of the young family, the 1901 ledgers from Thomson's General Store in Bognor indicate that "Tobacco," usually entered as "Tob," is by far the most frequent item purchased. Further inspection reveals that Dan rarely paid cash—he delivered cords of wood.

We have a copy of the Morrison family portrait, all nine of them, taken in front of our house, probably about 1910. In the back row is their first-born son, Neil (1889-1957)—always called Speely for reasons unknown. He is the only one wearing a cap and he has a bold and energetic look on his face. Father Dan sits stolidly in the front row, looking quizzical, knees and feet wide apart, working boots on, clothes shabby, flanked by daughters Edna and Donalda. Both girls' faces have been scratched out so all features are obliterated. Sarah, also sitting in the front row, looks pleased with the world and is wearing a long skirt, a blouse with leg-of-mutton sleeves, hair tautly drawn back. A "lovely lady" according to Frieda McKibbon's mother who used to visit the Morrison house as a child. Beside Sarah is their youngest son Russell (1900-1918). He would enlist with the 248th Battalion in February 1917, one of more than 630,000 Canadians recruited in that first world war. Wounded in service on October 26, 1918 at Cambrai, France, Russell would die of his wounds one month later. Three other children—Margaret, Angus (always called Pat) who stayed on the family farm and never married, and Christina (whose son Morrison Thomson gave us the Morrison photographs)—are also in the portrait.

A second portrait was obviously taken the same day. It shows Speely, Pat and Dan each holding a horse. Right behind them is the barn. And behind the barn, a stark hill, with not a tree to be seen. All three wear jackets as before. But the caps which Dan and Pat had removed for the family portrait have been put back on. Dan and Pat stand beside their horses, looking slightly more animated than in the family portrait. They look so ungainly, ties askew, jackets completely buttoned, hands hanging awkwardly at their sides, feet set apart. Speely presents a different image. His body language is confident, almost swaggering. He poses with one foot forward. Now we can see, as we could not in the family portrait, that he wears a dark turtleneck. His jacket is casually fastened by only one button. One hand rests nonchalantly in his trouser pocket while the other holds the bridle of the third horse. But Speely's face is not a happy one. He is looking away from the camera as though he wished he were somewhere else. The horses, two white-nosed Clydesdales and a skinny driving horse with ribs showing, are ungroomed and unkempt.

For the next twenty years Dan and his son Pat jointly owned the farm. It was a never-ending struggle for survival. The County Registry records show the property was mortgaged time after time. Every winter Pat and Speely used to go up north to cut logs in the bush. They must have been desperately trying to make ends meet.

Of all Dan Morrison's offspring, only one is still talked about by people from around Bognor, half admiringly, half disapprovingly: Speely, who married the much younger Mary Morrison (1897-1988) after (people still say) he got her "in the family way."

⁕⁕⁕⁕⁕

"LIFE IN YOUR HOUSE was real rough," said Dick. Both families, first the McArthurs and then the Morrisons, were known for "really hitting the bottle." That agreed with the stories Morrison Thomson told me. Morrison knew because he was Dan and Sarah's grandson. Some stories were amusing. How, as a remedy for bad stomachs, Speely and Pat were never without a pocketful of baking soda. Other stories were sad. How Dan's wife Sarah, fleeing from him when he was drunk and on the rampage, would climb up on a windowsill in the parlour and hide silently behind the heavy dark curtains, refusing to answer.

Dan Morrison was not a likeable character. At a time when horse-hair was used to make plaster and to pad upholstered furniture, solitary men drove wagons along country sideroads going from farm to farm to buy horse-hair. One such man came to the Morrison farm and Dan was happy to sell him a bag of horse-hair. Just as the transaction was concluded, Dan held the man back saying he had just remembered where he could find some more. Off Dan went, returning with a second bag. The driver paid for it, but when he returned to his wagon, he discovered that the second bag had been filled with hair from his own horse's tail, now completely shorn.

Dan and Sarah's sons, Pat and Speely, were, as Dick Murdoch recalled "always looking for an argument, always looking for a fight.

Speely wore spectacles without glass in them. He boasted that no one would start a fight with him if he was wearing glasses!" Betty said that she was "always afraid of Speely. He'd come to the house looking for a fight"—but she quickly added, "There's good in the worst of us and bad in the best."

Dick remembered one occasion when Speely's wife Mary called the police to the house because Speely was misbehaving. Whatever was happening must have simmered down, because the police were prepared to leave without taking Speely away. In those days, the lane from the house went straight up the hill to the road, exactly where Fred Miller had first shown me the house. Apparently the police did not want to go back up the steep lane to reach the top of the hill, so they asked Speely if there was another way out. Speely didn't hesitate. He directed the police in the general direction of the lane we currently use, running to the northwest around the base of the hill. But he set them just slightly off course. Speely warned that there was a damp spot just before they would get to the road. To get through it, the driver would have to gun the motor. Actually, Speely deliberately was directing them into the "swale" through which the old lane ran. The moment they drove into it, the police were well and truly stuck. "Speely made himself scarce," said Dick.

On another occasion when, as usual, too many people were drinking too much in the Morrison house, Speely decided he was dying of pneumonia. He phoned a doctor in Meaford, demanding a house call. When the doctor arrived he found Speely upstairs in bed. After examining him, the doctor agreed he did have pneumonia. "Well" said Speely, "if I'm going to die, I wanted to know the reason." The moment the doctor left, Speely rejoined the party downstairs—in spite of the diagnosis. He would live for many more years.

According to Dick, Speely was good at one thing: "Calling off the square dances at the hall—even though he was always drunk. And he'd get mad if the dancers didn't do it properly. He was always looking for an argument." Frieda McKibbon recalls that Speely was a very good dancer "*If* he could find someone to dance with him – which was hard because he was always loaded."

In 1929, Dan, Sarah and son Pat arranged a mortgage with the Ontario Loan and Debenture Co. Then in 1930, Pat sold the farm to Dan for the sum of $1.00. And in 1931, Dan Morrison's body was found somewhere between the house and the barn. Because Morrison fights were renowned—they could be heard on farms almost a mile away—it was generally believed he had died in a family fight. According to Dick, there was no investigation into Dan's death even though "there should've been." It is said that during Dan's funeral at McLean's cemetery, Speely stood by the grave shaking his head, muttering "No. Shouldn't've done it. No. Shouldn't've done it."

In March, 1933, the Supreme Court of Ontario became the grantor of the farm and the Ontario Loan and Debenture Co. became the grantee. Disbarred from any claim to the property were Sarah, Neil, Angus, Christina, Donalda and Edna. If the farm was their Utopia, they had lost it. "Losing the farm," the local euphemism for going bankrupt, happened to too many families on the Fifth Line.

When Frieda volunteered that "Speely was a very hard worker," I asked, why then the bankruptcy sale? "Just because you worked hard then, didn't mean you had any money," she retorted.

Lloyd Carmichael has an older brother, Ivan, who vividly remembers the bankruptcy sale on the Morrison farm. Speely didn't want to lose the farm equipment, so he hid it on Norman Smith's farm across the road from the Carmichael farm, about half a concession to the north and east. The auctioneer, Billy McKay, was Smith's brother-in-law, so when people noticed that there was much less equipment to sell than had been expected, the truth couldn't be hidden. All the men attending the sale took a short cut and walked across the fields to the Smith farm where the equipment was then auctioned off. It was this strange sight that so impressed Lloyd's brother.

After the bankruptcy sale, Speely moved in with his mother Sarah in Bognor. Why did the deaf and reclusive Sarah accept her middle-aged, renegade son into her Bognor home? The man who may have precipitated a stroke or heart attack in his elderly father? No one will ever know but I like to believe he came to her defence when she needed it.

Speely continued his alcohol-saturated existence. Jim Thomson, great-grandson of the founder of Thomson's General Store in Bognor, remembers "thrashing" as a boy in the 40s and 50s when Speely was still hiring himself out. "Speely always managed to be standing on top of the wagon." That, according to Jim, was the easiest job. On top of the wagon, all you had to do was stamp down the sheaves. Speely would taunt the young men down on the ground who had to throw the sheaves up on the wagon. "Can't you throw any higher than that?" he would jeer, and the young men would be goaded into throwing higher and higher.

In November, 1957, Speely died drunk in a car crash; he is buried in an unmarked grave in McLean's cemetery. His mother died three months later.

ALL THESE STORIES remain in people's memories. But what they usually talk about is the fun they had. How everyone made music—bagpipes, fiddles, pianos or singing. "Now you have to *hire* musicians," said Frieda disapprovingly. How much fun they had at dances! How skillfully clog dances and square dances and reels were performed! Forty years ago and more, dances were held every Saturday night in Bognor drawing people from Owen Sound and elsewhere. Many still go to dances regularly, wherever they may be—even if it means driving 45 minutes to Durham, or shorter trips to Walter's Falls, Bognor and Owen Sound.

Chapter 6

Town Rituals

Owen Sound has not awakened to the full value of its natural possessions.

Owen Sound on the Georgian Bay, Canada,
[Reesor, E.B.B., Thomson, N., 1912]

L IFE AT THE Hougues Magues has developed comfortable rituals
which we all enjoy. Town rituals happen mainly on Saturday
mornings. It would be a rare Saturday morning in town that
would not find us going to Fulford's Hardware which stands brazenly
orange on Owen Sound's main street, Second Avenue East. Founded in
the thirties by E.A. Fulford, the store in our time has been run by his
son, Jim Fulford, recently joined by his own son. In the early seventies,
the store was cool and dim when you entered and there was a musty,
astringent, mechanical odour to the place. Fulford's was all about the
practical realities of life, not the fripperies. Off to one side was a tinsmith and glazier's workroom. At the rear of the store there were huge
rolls of screening and wire and long racks of shovels, rakes, hoes and
brooms. Always, then and now, a huge display of machine tools—
drills, power saws, routers—that tempts Andrew and intimidates me.

The floors in the old store were bare wood and creaked as you
walked around. Commodious wooden drawers covered the walls

almost to the high ceiling, storing nails and spikes and hinges and other mysterious but necessary metallic objects. Wooden bins, which could be levered out, were under a massive wooden countertop, shiny and worn with years of use. A large and battered scale dangled over the counter, ready to weigh your order of spikes for nailing fence rails. Hung at eye level was a miscellany of objects to remind you of things you just might have forgotten you needed such as blank keys, key-chains, Vapona strips, sticky fly-catchers, paring knives and saw blades.

Now Fulford's Hardware has incorporated the adjoining store, more than doubling its floor area. There is a huge section for kitchen appliances and cooking equipment and another large section for bath-room fittings and fixtures. The centrepiece of the former store—the massive wooden counter—is no longer the focus of customer transactions. Instead, you pay for your purchases at a much less imposing island of cash registers, right where the wall separating the two stores used to be. But the friendliness remains.

Jim Fulford captured our loyalty as customers very soon after we arrived in Sydenham. Although we have yet to see water in our base-ment to the extent Norm McKibbon described, we do have minor waterfalls every spring (and sometimes after a heavy rain) running down the east wall of the basement nearest to the well. From there the water streams diagonally across Andrew's cement floor to the northwest corner. The first time we saw this we were understandably alarmed. Was our new furnace going to drown? Our unhappy discovery was made on a Wednesday around noon. A sump pump was what we need-ed and needed quickly. By now Norm had trained us to rely on Fulford's for everything. But in the early seventies, all the shops on Second Avenue closed on Wednesday at noon for a half-holiday. When Andrew phoned the store to find out whether they had a sump pump in stock, he caught Jim just as he was about to leave. No problem, Jim said, and waited while Andrew drove to Owen Sound. Astonishingly, that sump pump has now functioned for almost three decades, never failing to do its job.

It's not unusual to hear people remarking that Fulford's can be more expensive than some of its competitors. It's true, but Jim continues to get our business. His huge inventory includes all the things that major hardware chains don't stock because of small turnover. You can still purchase by the piece—as I did yesterday—one right-angled hook-screw for 10 cents, instead of being forced to buy a plastic box with 10 hooks in five different sizes that you don't need. What's more, I have often found that after hours of comparative shopping in Toronto to buy small kitchen appliances, supposedly at rock-bottom prices, I could have bought the same article for less at Fulford's. If you want small glass chimneys for the coal oil lamps, Fulford's will order them for you. If Jim doesn't have what you need, he'll tell you where to find it. And if you change your mind about something you've bought, Jim will take it back. For people who think hardware stores are fun stores to browse in, Fulford's is the place to go. In spite of all Jim's modernization, the old wooden drawers are still there and the floors still creak in the old part of the store.

❦

THE OWEN SOUND Farmers' Market, established in 1935, is a short walk from Fulford's through a parking lot. From our perspective, that parking lot is an opportunity waiting to be seized. On the east side, it is lined by the rear entrances to all the Second Avenue shops. On the west side of the parking lot, the Sydenham river flows on its way to Owen's Sound. On the far side of the river are trees and grassy banks where men and boys and black cormorants are often to be seen fishing. Also on the far side of the river are the large and gracious homes built at the end of the 19th century. Perhaps one day both sides of the river will take advantage of the natural beauty of the landscape. Instead of a dusty parking lot, will we someday see gardens and terraces, and residences and outdoor cafés? Owen Sound has yet to truly recognize the "full value of its natural possessions."

The Market operates out of a stolid, red brick building on Saturday mornings. No one knows when it was built, and no one is likely to find out because the old City Hall burnt down, destroying any records which might have documented the date. It may have been built in the mid-19th century to serve the railroad. From 1868 to 1935, the building was used as the Owen Sound Waterworks. Now, a covered arcade links the parking lot to the main entrance of the market building. In the winter, all the vendors are inside, but in the summer and fall, stalls are set up on both sides of the arcade. Here you can buy eggs, flowers, home-baked cookies, cake and bread, cut flowers, garden plants, fresh and smoked fish caught by First Nations fishermen from Cape Croker, vegetables, honey, fruit, birdseed, place-mats, planters, canes and brooms. As long as the weather remains mild, young local musicians play everything from country to baroque music.

But the heart of the market over the course of all seasons is inside, because there you find the vendors who can be counted on all year round. Every week you can buy the best fresh fish—splake, whitefish or trout—from Howell's, an enterprise started in the early fifties by the late Mary Howell and her husband Lloyd, a man apparently more trouble than he was worth. Her story in *Born Running: Reminiscences of Mary Howell* documents how someone born without a silver spoon in her mouth and in spite of much adversity, achieved success. Mary's sister Beth and her sister-in-law Penny still stand behind the counter week after week, deftly wrapping fish in newspaper, always ready to add some ice if it's hot outside. And most Saturdays we stand in the long lineup to buy fresh fish for dinner at the Hougues Magues.

Andrew's Lake Trout with Sorrel

This is a recipe for cooks who do not need precise quantities! What follows would be for 4 servings.

In a frying pan, sauté one chopped shallot or a small onion in some butter. Then wash, drain and chiffonade 1 cup sorrel and

1 cup lettuce, Swiss chard or spinach fresh from the garden.
Cook the greens over a low heat in butter for one minute with
the cooked shallots. If desired, 1-2 tbsp whipping cream can
be added at the end. Peel, seed and cube half an English
cucumber, and add some chopped chervil and a vinaigrette
dressing. Cook fish in butter over a medium heat, allowing
10 minutes per inch of thickness.

When the fish is cooked, each serving is placed in the center of
the plate, on top of the warm greens. The cucumber mixture is placed
on each side as a garnish. Very often we have this after a first course of
pasta, such as ravioli, in which case only stir-fried vegetables, perhaps
carrots and broccoli, are served with the fish course.

Ravioli with Sage, Parmesan and Butter

This too is a recipe without precise quantities. It's good for lunch
with a salad, or for a first course at dinner. We buy large frozen ravioli, preferring cheese-filled rather than meat. (Fresh pasta seems more
inclined to disintegrate when being cooked.)

Put frozen pasta into boiling water in a large saucepan. Cook
until done, in the quantity you require. Four pieces
per serving is the maximum most people can eat for a lunch
and three is more than enough for a first course. They are
very filling. When cooked, garnish with fresh sage leaves from the
garden. The sage is for eating! Add shaved curling slices
of Parmesan cheese. For each serving, pour at least 2 tbsp
of melted butter over sage and cheese.

Another feature of the Owen Sound Farmers' Market is the
butcher counter which sells beef, sausages, ham and cold cuts, but best
of all is the meaty bacon—not the plastic-packaged-water-saturated-
slimy bacon that's sold in supermarkets with a best-before date of six
weeks. Buying bacon in this cholesterol-obsessed age does give me

twinges of guilt, so we try to buy it not more than once a month, sometimes twice if we have company. We have three favourite ways of using it, two of which are lunches. Cooked until it's crisp and tender, not crisp and brittle, it's wonderful with fried Portobello mushrooms, a salad and good bread. It's equally wonderful with sliced, ripe, field-grown tomatoes, mayonnaise and lettuce, again on good bread toasted or otherwise. When I make these sandwiches, I cut the bacon slices in thirds before cooking them. It's easier to distribute the bacon over the whole sandwich and it certainly makes it easier to eat.

The third way we like the bacon is with a French Toast Casserole.

Hougues Magues French Toast with Blueberries

It's very convenient when you have a crowd for breakfast, to make this the night before. However, if it's for a late brunch it can be prepared the same morning provided there will be at least two hours standing time before it goes in the oven. If you freeze your own blueberries in the summer, you can make this dish any time of the year. Beware of commercial frozen blueberries in syrup. They don't work.

Remove crusts from half-inch slices of bread, preparing sufficient to provide two layers of bread for a 9x13 inch pan. You can use baguettes or Italian bread for greater density than a sandwich loaf. Beat together 4 eggs, 1/2 cup milk, 1/4 tsp baking powder and 1 tsp vanilla. Pour over bread. Cover with plastic wrap. Refrigerate overnight. One half hour before serving, mix 4 1/2 cups blueberries (I sometimes use less) with 1/2 cup sugar, 1 tsp cinnamon and 1 tsp cornstarch. Grease a second 9x13 inch pan. (If you do not have two such pans, carefully remove wet slices of bread from the first pan, rinse and dry it, grease it with butter and reuse it.) Spread the blueberry mixture in the pan. Then put the moistened bread on top. Brush surface with 2 tbsp melted butter. Bake at 450°F for 25 minutes.

Inside the market you can sometimes find locally grown Shiitake and oyster mushrooms, more eggs (even duck eggs) and more vegetables. Air-chilled chicken for roasting. Delicately smoked and tender boneless chicken breasts. Delicious chicken pies, great for quick meals or emergency entertaining. There is always a choice of dessert pies, including the familiar range of fruit pies and one unusual entry—a covered lemon pie filled with paper-thin slices of lemons in a custardy sauce. The Pickle Guy sells relishes and pickles. Others sell jams, locally made greeting cards, children's clothes, superb lamb, breads, wreaths, flower arrangements, pottery, jewellery, knitted goods, treacle tarts, tourtières, steak and kidney pies, lasagna, pizza, fresh pasta and even Chinese food. The variety is extraordinary. As we make our way slowly through the two crowded aisles, we meet familiar faces and stop to chat, which inevitably blocks traffic flow. If there is a lot to talk about and we don't have a large crowd to feed at lunch, we arrange to meet later a local café for morning coffee.

ANOTHER TOWN RITUAL is shopping for our Toronto groceries in Owen Sound. People are amazed that we do this, but it's much more pleasant and much less time-consuming to shop there on a Saturday morning compared to dealing with traffic, scarce parking and long lineups in Toronto stores, especially during the week after a long day at work.

Still other town rituals have come and gone. There used to be a huge second-hand shop on Second Avenue East. Our weekend guests were as eager as we were to make it our first stop on Saturday mornings. The proprietor eventually lost interest in attending enough house sales, garage sales and farm auctions to maintain a large inventory. But before she closed shop, we and our friends had fun snapping up an astonishing array of glass, china, silver plate, furniture and art quite inexpensively.

Then there used to be McKay Brothers Ltd., a dry goods store on Second Avenue East, established in 1905. It's gone now, but we took all our Hougues Magues visitors there until it closed. The store had two main attractions. The first was a money monorail, an amazing mechanical contraption that took money from the customer on the main floor and whirred it up on a system of wires to the second floor where any change due was put back into the metal cylinder and whirred right back to the customer. It was fascinating to watch. The second attraction at McKay's was a row of female wax heads, with smooth pastel complexions, nostalgically-styled human hair and sweetly benign expressions. Protected in a curving glass-fronted oak cabinet and viewing the world from a level of no more than 18 inches above the floor, these disconcerting beings mutely displayed scarves and jewellery. They were so ladylike! My mother could remember when Eaton's had had similar displays in the twenties.

We take our business to Parker's Pharmacy, to Seupersaud's paint and wallpaper store, to the local picture framer, and to the Ginger Press where you can book-browse or drink coffee after shopping at the market. Parker's was founded in 1856 by John Parker, who emigrated from Yorkshire, England. He also established pharmacies in Durham, Goderich, Elora and Chatsworth. His successor, Stephen Johnston Parker found time to be Grey County Treasurer, and to be involved with the Board of Trade, the Owen Sound Waterworks, the Owen Sound Telephone Company and the Gas Company.

Now, Parker's in Owen Sound is owned by a local partnership, one of whom, Peter Rissi is a superb musician. He obligingly rounds up players from within a hundred-mile radius to perform everything from Big Band to jazz to polkas, as required. He can be found playing anywhere—on cruises in the bay, in halls, in private gardens, and in tents, as happened in the summer of 1998 when Nigel and Caroline were married at the farm.

Colbert Seupersaud, originally from Guyana, is a house painter by trade who knows everything about paints and how to apply them. Like many others we have met, he is helpful beyond belief. After some minor renovations to the kitchen, I wanted to re-hang wallpaper I had carefully removed before the job started, but I was convinced I couldn't do it. Colbert came to the rescue, pasting and hanging it for me. He then lectured me at great length on how you must never rely on pre-pasted wallpaper, and made me promise that in the future I would always put on paste before hanging. He went further and insisted on lending me his wide brushes so I could apply wallpaper paste properly. Later, when we were uncertain which shade of white for the new crown moulding would match the white ceiling and new wallpaper, Colbert drove to the house to advise us. Years of climbing ladders eventually finished Bert's knees, so he and his wife Barbara invested in a paint store on Second Avenue East. After they retire, I'll keep on bothering them for advice, so they are duly warned.

❧

EVERY SO OFTEN we are reminded that we are still outsiders. It has been said that Owen Sound does not to take too kindly to those who are not third generation Owen Sounders. In this way it resembles small cities everywhere. Unlike other Ontario cities and towns such as Port Hope, Goderich, Elora and Southampton, Owen Sound has done little to exploit its stunningly beautiful physical setting. Nor has it taken advantage of its late 19th and early 20th century commercial and industrial streetscapes, with the exception of two very attractive restored storefronts on Second Avenue East. And so much more could be done with the shorelines and river banks.

Owen Sound's deep-rooted, no-nonsense pragmatism is revealed by its street names—all numbers, with streets going east/west and avenues going north/south. Owen Sound used to have streets with real names, names that evoked its history and the people who shaped it. Sadly, history was obliterated without a moment of regret or awareness.

Convenience may have been achieved, but at the cost of diluting a sense of place.

But there are consolations. Owen Sound's Tom Thomson Memorial Art Gallery is superb. There is an excellent library, a fascinating museum, a shrine to Billy Bishop, the World War I ace, the spacious and beautiful Harrison park, a local orchestra and the restored Roxy Theatre, site of many plays and concerts. Each year, to mark the Christmas season, a sparkling winter wonderland is installed along the banks of the river. A true Festival of Lights, it presents a panorama of winter themes which is quite magical after darkness has fallen. And meetings are in progress to explore ways to re-vivify downtown Owen Sound. There is much to be grateful for and enough reason for optimism.

Chapter 7

Spring Rituals

*The principle of private landownership and the possessiveness it fostered
ensured that fencing would flourish in Southern Ontario.*

**Thomas McIlwraith in *Looking for Old Ontario*.
University of Toronto Press. 1997.**

S EASONAL RITUALS are the essence of life on a farm and the
beginning season is spring. First heralded long before the snow
disappears by the yellowing of the willows, the next thing we
notice is the sound of rushing water spilling down the creek. As early
as February snowdrops appear. A little later, when it's still uncom-
fortably cold, iris reticulata, four to six inches high and intensely purple emerge in the garden, and then in March come the white, yellow
and purple crocuses. Before the trees have a chance to release their
leaves, white and pink trilliums reflecting shafts of sunlight spread
over the forest floors, most luxuriantly in the roadside woods on the
fifth line just north of our farm. By late April, boisterously yellow
marsh marigolds erupt wherever marshy ground exists—the first
pickable wildflowers to bring into the house. Tiny white and purple
violets are easily overlooked in our woods. Our garden fills with stately daffodils some white, others a range of yellows and oranges, many
the progeny of bulbs my uncle, Theo van Erk gave us in our early
years at the Hougues Magues.

Then come dainty pink-flowering honeysuckle and the lilacs, some long resident on the farm and some new varieties which we planted. Massive clumps of white, purple and mauve lilacs, often ten feet high, wide and deep, are seen throughout southern Ontario every spring. In the past, every farm must have had lilacs. The lilacs have outlasted many farms, becoming evidence that a house used to be here and is no more. As Andrew Armitage points out in his book *Owen Sound: The Day the Governor Came to Town and Other Tales*, Sydenham had no lilacs before the settlers came. Lilacs were brought in by the settlers, a symbol of domestication, and planted for luck. They were planted beside the house, in front of the house, and sometimes by outdoor privies. Some still believe that lilacs are best left outdoors, unpicked. As cut flowers, or even worse, worn on a lapel, lilacs may bring misfortune, white lilacs more so than purple. On our farm there were and are no white lilacs. Only purple.

As the lilacs fade in our garden, the peonies and the iris and the early roses take over. In the pinewoods behind the house, rhododendrons bloom. We never would have thought of planting them, had it not been for the urging of a neighbour whose passion was rhododendrons. Spring after spring, our pleasure increases. But before very long, the lawn needs cutting and there are so many other things we want to do, we simply cannot do them all.

Michael, our son-in-law, has become custodian of the lilacs, and in late spring every year, he climbs up a ladder and deadheads all the withered lilac blooms. I deadhead the peonies, the daffodils, the tulips and early roses, and prune back shrubs to shape them and remove winter-killed branches. Nickie weeds and Andrew divides perennials, plants new specimens, gets the vegetable garden started and patiently provides me with loads of mulch which I demand for the trees in the garden.

One of the much-loved features of the Caledon Lake cottage was a graceful willow that shaded the dock. It's no surprise then that one of the first trees we ever planted in the garden was a willow. Its branches started two more willow trees which would grow luxuriously at the edge of our big pond and eventually be ruthlessly felled by beavers. But before that happened, Michael indulged his mother-in-law. Using only branches cut from these willows, he planted what would become an avenue of willows along the creek bed near the house. Each spring he inspects them for winter damage, usually due to mice nibbling the bark, and then prunes them in a unique manner, making them look like maples from a distance. Now the willows are sufficiently numerous to withstand any beaver attack, unless a whole platoon arrives.

Other spring tasks are more onerous. Repairing fences. Planting trees. Stone-picking. In comparison, bringing in our first harvest is no challenge at all.

INITIALLY, FENCING took priority over tree planting. The right time for building fences is the spring when the sun is not too hot and the black flies, mosquitoes and deer flies have not yet come out to torment human beings. Most importantly, the ground is still wet and soft, so it is relatively easy to dig holes for fence posts. Mechanical post-hole diggers are available, but they don't work in stony soil! We began by winding up yards and yards of broken and rusted barbed wire into dozens of coils. It all had to be taken to the township dump, along with vast rolls of unused, rusty pagewire fencing which previous owners had dumped in the creek bed. I still detest rusty wire of any kind.

Mistakenly, we concluded that shiny new barbed wire was just what we wanted, even though stretching it tightly from post to post or from post to tree with a wire stretcher was hard work and always unpredictably hazardous because so often the wire snapped as we stretched it. After several winters we learned that heavy snow breaks even new barbed wire and the new wire that didn't break inevitably rusted. Old-fashioned cedar fence rails were infinitely preferable to barbed wire. When rail fences collapse under the weight of snow, it's easy to resurrect them in the spring, and to replace broken rails. All this is possible *if* you have a supply of cedar fence rails. We were lucky. We were given some and were able to buy more.

There are many ways to build rail fences. The snake-rail fence uses lots of rails, but no nails are necessary. The rails go zig and zag, overlapping generously. This is a rather extravagant approach, using too many rails and too much land, but it's easy to build and move, and is easily repaired.

A post-and-rail fence uses pairs of fence posts set about six inches apart, encircled with wire about ten inches above the ground. The rails are placed between the paired fence posts alternately. Imagine four pairs of fence posts (pairs one, two, three and four). The first rail is dropped between pairs two and three and rests on the wire. The second rail is dropped between pairs one and two; and the third between pairs three and four. The fourth would go between pairs two and three on top of the first rail—and so you would continue down a whole fence line until you have four or five rails between each pair of posts. With time of course, the paired posts would gradually splay apart in a useless V and the rails would collapse. To prevent this from happening, the fence builder must wire together each pair of fence posts at two or preferably three levels. So as well as bringing fence rails, shovel and posts, the fence builder must be equipped with rolls of strong wire, wire cutters, and pliers as well as a chain saw to trim the rails at the site. Strong muscles are needed to twist and tighten the loops of wire encircling the pairs of posts as the rails stack up. This type of fence makes more efficient use of the fence rails, but it is much less easy to repair than a snake-rail fence.

The third method is to nail rails on single fence posts. It guarantees that forearms will get sore and even swollen because of the effort of hammering six- and eight-inch spikes through the rails. The rails can break over the winter and the fence posts, particularly on hills, have an unwelcome habit of leaning over. And it is always a

Boulder fence-rows.

nuisance finding the right length of rail for any of the three methods; they inevitably seem too long or too short.

Tree stumps, with their excavated halos of radiating roots, were also used by the settlers to make fences when they cleared the land. An uprooted tree stump tilted on its side formed an effective barrier for livestock but it wasted a lot of land. It's not a method we ever used.

Stones make fences too. Rows of stones, piled two to three feet high, the result of decades of stone-picking, can be seen all over the farm. But such a "fence" will not hold back livestock wanting to get into the field on the other side of the fence. The best way, the most laborious way, the most back-breaking way to make fences is to erect dry stone walls. Some of the early settlers were very skillful at constructing them. Once built, they should last forever. A few can be found on our farm (exactly where we do not need them) and others are still to be found elsewhere in Grey County. Nigel and Andrew both became enamoured of building dry stone walls. It is a sacrifice when, in his limited time at the farm, Nigel builds and repairs rail fences, because his heart is in building stone walls. To build stone walls is both mentally and physically challenging. Choosing the right stone and finding the right place for it so it will not jiggle is not an easy job. Over the years both Nigel and Andrew have learned how to make a very good dry stone wall. They are getting better all the time, but it really is a job for young backs.

One more kind of fence remains—a pagewire fence. We decided to put one up along the road, the fifth line, at the front of our property. For this we needed help. One of the neat things about working with people we hired, is that we learned a lot about how people rooted in rural Ontario look at the world. The individual we engaged to put in the fence-posts (who shall go nameless) was eager to share his wisdom with us while we worked together. "People are stupid," he said. "They think if tax money pays for it, it's free." He went on, "if we lose this country, it's our fault." I agreed with him on the latter point then and still do. Later on I wrote in my diary: *We got 32 posts in. It was pouring. We returned to the house, boots full of water, soaked and dripping to the skin. Then the rain stopped and the sun came out.* We weren't thrilled when we got our bill from this rural philosopher. It was for four days' labour, when he'd done only two. Nor were we thrilled when a neighbour who came to help us stretch the pagewire and fix it to the posts, said the fence-posts had been very badly put in.

The saying goes, "good fences good neighbours make." There is nothing like owning a farm to make one realize how true that is. Up until the seventies, all our boundary fences were divvied up between the owners of our farm and the owners of the three adjacent farms. Each spring, no reminders needed, each owner repaired the section of the fence for which he was responsible. This is no longer always the case. Who wants to build fences if they have no livestock? So some new landowners just do all the fencing, even though they should be responsible for only 50 per cent of the fences bordering their property. However, you don't really have much choice if you want to avoid visits from livestock you don't own. Fences are essential.

In 1982 we arrived one weekend in early July to discover that a whole herd of cattle from a farm more than two kilometres away had visited our garden. Unfortunately, before their owner retrieved them, the cattle had destroyed a plum tree, three maples, a linden tree, a lilac, a mountain ash, a cinquefoil, two Chinese almonds, two Russian olives and many cedars. They broke a glass lawn table, tore down eavestroughs, upturned the picnic bench, ate all our flowers and most of our vegetables, broke fence rails, broke fence wire and pulled ivy down from the wall. This does provide an incentive to maintain fences. However, even with good fences and properly closed gates, we had another unwelcome visit in 1993. This time only three heifers arrived, but they had strayed even further from home. Our visitors broke our gazing globe, overturned the birdbath, and enjoyed the usual repast of flowers and vegetables.

Of course, the truth is that no fence will hold back a herd of spooked cattle. They will charge through anything. Sometimes it's lightning and sometimes it's flies that set them off. Even when cattle are not spooked, they have a talent for finding the single gap in a long fence, the one place with two weak rails, the one place where the bottom rail is high enough that they can nose under it. Inspecting fences is an important spring rite.

WE PLOUGHED, fertilized and seeded our fields with green manure and grain because of our commitment to improving our agricultural land. We ended up planting as much trefoil—both better and more expensive than clover—as we could afford. But ploughing, while it did discourage weeds and hawthorns, also brought to the surface stones, stones and more stones. So with our friend Don Emmerson,

"Stoning machine," used to remove stones from fields, 1902.
With permission from County of Grey–Owen Sound Museum.

whose farm is one concession south of us and who eventually took over our pasture after Norm retired from farming, we tackled a chore long familiar to Sydenham farmers. Stone-picking. Every spring for more than a century, stones were picked from the fields and dumped on the stone fence-rows at the edge of the fields. Stones are an unwanted but predictable crop, just like weeds. Some have speculated why stones come up to the surface every spring. The explanations centre on relative cold and heat, and push versus pull. It's probably true that the soil above and below a stone will retain cold longer than soil free of stones. Does the cold earth above the stone pull it towards the surface? Does thawed earth encroach under the stone and push it up? Whatever the mechanism, stones come up every spring.

There appeared to be three systems for collecting stones: the apron system, the hand-held bucket and the front-end loader. With an apron, women could collect a dozen or more of the smaller stones and dump them on the fence-row. Stones could also be lugged to the fence-row in a bucket. Infinitely preferable was a tractor equipped with a front-end loader. It followed the stone-pickers, men, women and children, as they went up and down the fields clunking in the stones. It was almost fun.

We wanted to reforest the remaining 65 acres of land. Norm definitely did not approve. He knew our steep slopes were hazardous and unsuited for agricultural use in the last half of the 20th century. He remembered when the "dogs" failed and fully loaded wagons broke loose, careening down hills, in one instance almost colliding with the house. It was Frieda who explained that "the dogs weren't human dogs." They were mechanical devices which held the wagon halfway up a hill so that tired horses could have a rest. "Shoes" were what braked wagons coming down the hill, according to Frieda. Much of our hilly farm put tractors and their drivers at risk, as even the very cautious Don Emmerson would find out.

Years ago Norm had scraped the gravelly soil on the hill right behind the Hougues Magues in a fruitless attempt to mine gravel. That failed gravel pit remained an eyesore when we arrived. Nevertheless, from Norm's point of view, reforestation would undo the labour of the first settlers and be a betrayal. With only axes and handsaws (and fire), they had cleared the land of virgin forest, a struggle we can hardly imagine. But this was one time we ignored Norm's advice. Much, but not all of the land went back to trees.

In the early seventies, the provincial government wanted to encourage reforestation in southern Ontario as an antidote to thousands of acres of neglected land which had been cleared and was now totally unsuited for agriculture. In the short term, reforestation would stop erosion, encourage wildlife and enhance retention of water. In the long term, it would renew an important natural resource, timber. Managed forest agreements were established involving the Ministry of

Natural Resources and individual landowners who then benefited in many ways. (So did porcupines. They moved in very quickly and have since dined splendidly in the treetops where they live.) A ministry forester did site inspections and made recommendations as to what should be planted and where. It happened that our first forester was overly keen on monoculture, suggesting we plant only white pine. The problem with monoculture is that if white pines were knocked off by a disease, then our whole new forest would be affected. So we requested that diverse species be planted by the ministry, including white, red and jack pine, ash, maple, poplar, black and Norway spruce, and cedar. In 1980 we would surprise our ministry advisors by suggesting larch trees should be planted on our steep slopes. They would grow rapidly, but being shallow-rooted, larches can keel over with high winds or after heavy snowfalls.

Now we remember with some bemusement how one of our first ministry consultants assured us that the white pine weevil never attacked trees after they reached 12 to 14 feet in height. Our white pine forest demonstrates how wrong he was. The damage the weevil larvae do results in the trunks forking so that instead of one tall trunk, there is a tight Y formed and two trunks continue to grow upward, reducing considerably the future value of the tree. A majority of our white pines were hit when they were 20 feet high, a time when you can no longer remedy the problem. Obviously, if we had accepted monoculture, our entire population of trees would have been damaged. As it is, just some of our trees have been affected.

The first Ontario Government grant we received in the early seventies had been for the removal of diseased and dead elm trees. In the same period we benefited from a ministry program which sent in a team of tree planters to plant as many as 10,000 trees in a season. Landowners paid for the trees which came from ministry-owned nurseries, but they did not have to pay for the labour associated with planting them. Landowners could also buy extra trees if they wanted to plant any themselves. So in the fall, we would order trees from the nursery for spring pick-up. Each spring for around 15 years I would drive an hour cross-country to pick up 1000 to 1500 trees—Carolina poplars, cedar, black locusts, red oak, black walnut and others—which we would then plant ourselves, often with the help of friends. In 1984 our list was: silver maple (200), larch (200), poplar (100), white pine (100), cedar (200), Scotch pine (50), white spruce (100) and Norway spruce (150). We would plant all the trees in one weekend.

There is a right way to plant trees. We carried 20 to 30 young trees, about 12 to 15 inches long, in a bucket, damp moss protecting the roots. Andrew pushed the shovel as deeply as possible into the ground (our neighbours always called it "dirt") and then leaned forward on the handle to open up a wedge-shaped space. I would thrust a tree into the space, holding it in while Andrew removed the shovel. Andrew went on to the next site and I would use the heel of my boot to shut the wedge and close the space. Then on to join Andrew. Three or four of us, friends and family, would do 1000 or more trees in a weekend. The professional planters did the job much more quickly than we could. Hard work, especially when it rained, but gratifying.

Often a large proportion of newly planted trees can die. We have been unusually lucky, experiencing virtually no loss at all. Young trees are very vulnerable. If they had been allowed to dry out before they were planted, or if they were planted carelessly and not well heeled in, or if they were planted too late in the spring when the earth was dry and no rain came, the loss could be up to 80 per cent. We had almost a 100 per cent take with the exception of one small triangular slope to the north of the creek where we planted year after year without any success. Finally we realized that we were planting trees that did not like wet feet. It turned out that silver maple and white spruce were what were needed and they have grown well.

Even with relatively ideal conditions, growth in the first few years after planting is slow. This phenomenon is very easy to see in white pines. Every year, a single candle-like shoot, the leader, thrusts upward at the top of the tree. (It is the leader that the pine weevil attacks.) The following year, branches extend laterally like spokes of a wheel from the tip of last year's candle, and another candle extends upward. The space between each circle or layer of branches represents one year's growth. In early years and bad years, the space between one layer of branches and the next is small. With increasing age, the space increases—up to three feet, which is phenomenal growth in one year. By counting the number of spaces between the layers of branches, you can tell how old a tree is. Looking at our trees, it's obvious that during the first three to five years, growth was as little as six inches per year. By years seven or eight, the trees did achieve three-foot growth annually, but this maximum growth never occurs in every tree in every year. There were good years and bad years, and ever in good years, there were many different micro-environments.

Given all the ministry services (and benefits such as a property tax rebate for the managed forest), it was only fair that the landowner had defined responsibilities. First the landowner had to keep livestock away from the trees. Cattle tamp down the earth and damage the tree roots close to the surface. Cattle also eat young undergrowth—the new saplings needed for forest renewal. Rapidly growing white pines are supposed to serve as nursemaids to young maple saplings which self-seed among the pines. Because of the taller pine trees around them, the maples are forced to grow straight and ever taller to reach the sunlight. Fences are necessary to prevent cattle from interfering with this cycle. The landowner was also supposed to inspect the trees for disease and report back to the ministry as soon as any problems appeared.

The ministry not only helped us with reforesting, it also advised us on how to manage our established woodlot with its many mature trees. Our ministry forester inspected the forest and, with yellow spray paint, marked "weed trees" such as ironwood. He also marked diseased or malformed trees, and trees which had to be sacrificed because they were too close to another tree to allow them both to flourish. Then, again with ministry advice, we arranged for the marked trees to be cut for saw logs with the tops producing about 40 cords of firewood. This gave us a small amount of revenue for the farm. It also cleared space for the crowns of remaining trees, allowing them to spread and prosper.

However, not everyone was favourably disposed towards the Ministry of Natural Resources. One local cynic (along with many others) claimed the ministry was "in the pocket of industry. The MNR tells us all to plant white pine. We look after them. We pay taxes on them. In 15 years, our only customer for white pine will be Company X. The MNR does everything to make it convenient for the company." As for girdling trees as the MNR recommended at that time, our source went on, "It's a crime against humanity. All that solar energy going to waste. Besides, it helps spread disease to have all those dying trees in the woods." He claimed that it was the ministry that had put in beaver to the north of us, and he predicted the beavers were going to be an awful problem. "It's a good thing the MNR isn't our enemy when you see how mean and nasty they are as our friends." A different point of view—but the beavers have become a problem.

THE FIRST FOUR or five years after you plant, it seems nothing is happening and you wonder if you will ever see the fruits of your labour. Then, all of a sudden, the young trees are higher than the surrounding vegetation and become very obvious. By the time two decades have passed the trees can be in excess of 30 feet tall. Ski trails that traversed bare and windy fields in the seventies now are sheltered by tall trees, secure from piercing wind. The lane from the road to the house was open and windswept when we bought the farm. Now it goes through a tall pine and spruce mini-forest, protected from stormy blast in the winter and shaded in the summer. The original woodlot at the back of the farm has flourished following the removal of undesirable trees. Today when we see our tall trees covering so much of the land, it's hard to believe the land was so barren when we arrived.

We don't plant trees anymore; we've filled all the available spaces. The time has come again to selectively cut them.

GIANT-LEAFED RHUBARB is the first harvest of the year. It grows so rapidly it's a challenge to get it picked while the pink stalks are still slim and tender. The rhubarb can be cut up in 2-inch pieces and frozen for future use (as in rhubarb and black currant jam in the next chapter), or it can be stewed gently for a breakfast fruit. Best of all it can be made into

Ruth Carmichael's Rhubarb Custard Pie

Prepare an unbaked 9-inch pie shell and 3 cups fresh rhubarb cut in 1-inch pieces. Mix 4 tbsp flour in 1 1/2 cups sugar and combine with 2 tbsp soft butter. Add sugar mixture to 2 beaten eggs and beat. Put rhubarb in pie shell and pour egg mixture over the fruit. Bake at 450°F for 20 minutes and then reduce heat to 350°F. Bake until the custard is set.

As for the unbaked pie shell, the cook has two choices. One is to buy frozen unbaked pie shells at the supermarket, and the other is to make your own. When I first got married, I despaired of ever mastering the art of making piecrusts. My mother's pastry was made with lard, and Andrew's mother used shortening. Their pies were wonderful. Meticulous compliance with either of their recipes in my hands led to sticky, unrollable pastry which, if I patted it together in the pie pan, resulted in a tough cardboard.

Finally I found a recipe that has served me well ever since. This recipe produces enough crust for three pies. When I make it, I cut off one third for immediate use and freeze the remainder. When it's time to use the frozen pastry, it should be thawed overnight in the refrigerator.

Hougues Magues Pie Crust

In a large bowl place 3 1/2 cups all-purpose flour and 1/2 tsp salt. Add 8 1/2 oz (just over 1 cup) shortening and 3 oz (6 tbsp) butter, both frozen, cut into small pieces. (Alternatively, frozen lard may be used. Having recently read how lard is made, I am not eager to use it.) Using a pastry blender, cut the flour and fat mixture until it has the texture of coarse meal. Add 1 cup very cold water and mix thoroughly, first with the pastry blender and then using your hands to form into a ball. Roll out the ball on a floured board to make a rectangle about 18 x 6 inches. Fold in thirds and roll out again. Fold in thirds, wrap in cling wrap and chill in refrigerator for an hour. Cut off about one third of the pastry, which will be sufficient to make two pie shells or one pie with a top. Freeze the remainder in a tightly sealed plastic bag for future use.

Another way to use up rhubarb is to bake a cake. A frequent guest at the Hougues Magues has now forgotten that many years ago she brought us the following cake.

Bev Harris's Rhubarb Coffee Cake

Grease 13" x 9" pan and heat oven to 350°F. For topping, mix together 1/4 cup butter, 2 tsp cinnamon and 3/4 cup brown sugar. Sift together 2 cups sifted all-purpose flower with 1 tsp soda and 1/2 tsp salt. Cream together 1/2 cup butter and 1 1/4 cups sugar. Beat in 1 egg and 1 tsp vanilla. Add dry ingredients alternately with 1 cup buttermilk (beginning and ending with dry ingredients) mixing as minimally as possible. Add 2 cups chopped rhubarb to which has been added 1 tbsp flour. Pour into cake pan. Sprinkle topping on the batter. Bake for 45 minutes or until done. Can be cut into up to 18 squares.

Chapter 8

Summer Rituals

*The blood is sometimes streaming from you in various directions
before you are aware that you are much bitten…The mosquitoes will bite
through almost anything and the black flies are most ingenious
in finding their way through all defences…*

Letter from Anne Langton, July 7, 1839.

SOMETIMES SUMMER would begin before spring had ended. The first sign would be an invitation from Ruth Carmichael to go strawberry picking. Local farmers with huge fields of strawberries put out radio and newspaper advertisements when their berries are ripe. The slogan is "Pick your own," although you can always go to the farmhouse and buy quarts of picked berries at a slightly higher price than when you pick your own. Sensible pickers prefer to go in early to mid-morning after the berries have dried off from the night's dampness but before the sun becomes mercilessly hot, and also before the best strawberries have been picked off. This was never a man's job. Neither was it much liked by young boys, who if present, assuaged their injured pride by eating almost as many strawberries as they put into the boxes.

The children and I would set off equipped with hats, quart boxes (preferably wooden ones, not cardboard) saved from the previous year, and "flats." The flats hold eight quart-sized boxes tight together which allows much higher heaping than is possible with free-standing quart boxes, a skill I learned from Ruth. If we were lucky we'd find a tree to park under. Then, containers in hand, we'd proceed in dusty heat to the strawberries. Before starting to pick, we carefully inspected the rows of plants, looking for the ideal spot. We wanted the row with the reddest and most plentiful strawberries. While it was much quicker to fill a quart from a small section of one row, often, since we were choosy, we would go from one row to another, to get the most appealing berries. The only limitation was field etiquette. Poaching on a row where someone else was already picking would be inexcusable.

By the time the berries were paid for and we returned to the car, it would be suffocatingly hot. Even though the pickers were weary, there was no respite, because as soon as we got home (car and house had no air-conditioning), the strawberries, warm from both the heat of the sun and the car, required immediate attention. After washing and hulling them (making our fingers even more stained), some would be frozen on cookie sheets and later stored in plastic bags, some would be used for jam, and some would be reserved for strawberry shortcake for dessert that evening.

Freezer Strawberry Jam

No cooked jam can equal the colour and the fresh taste of this jam which is made with Certo, a commercially available fruit pectin sold in pouches of liquid or in boxes of powder. Its disadvantage is that the jam keeps only if frozen. Stored in the fridge it lasts about three weeks. The recipe comes as an insert in the Certo box and it goes something like this:

> Crush sufficient cleaned strawberries to yield 1 3/4 cups. Do not use over-ripe fruit. Mix four cups of sugar into the berries and let stand for 10 minutes. Add 2 tbsp lemon juice and 1 pouch Certo liquid, stirring for three minutes. Pour into jars, filling to within 1/2 inch of top. Cover with lids and let stand at room temperature until set. This may take up to 24 hours. Store in freezer.

As for strawberry shortcake, people now seem to buy prepackaged, flat yellow cakes in the supermarket. But in our family, there is only one way we want to eat strawberry shortcake.

Hougues Magues Strawberry Shortcake

There is no question that last-minute baking is essential for best results. Everything can be prepared ahead of time up to the point where the liquid will be added to the flour mixture. Then the recipe can easily be completed about 20 to 30 minutes before you plan to serve dessert.

Also do-able in advance is the cleaning of the strawberries. There cannot be too many. Their flavour is enhanced by halving small strawberries and quartering large ones and then sprinkling them with sugar, a tiny pinch of white pepper and a dash of balsamic vinegar.

Sift into mixing bowl 2 cups sifted all-purpose flour with 3 tsp baking powder, 3/4 tsp salt and 4 tbsp sugar. Add grated rind of one lemon. Put 1/2 cup of butter with flour mixture, and using pastry cutter, chop until the mixture is well blended but still crumbly. Add one beaten egg and 1/4 cup of milk and mix first with fork and then with fingers to make a ball of dough. Place dough on greased cookie sheet and make a circle 9" in diameter. Score surface with knife to make 4, 6 or 8, wedge shaped servings. Bake in 450°F oven for 10-15 minutes—the cake should be no more than golden brown. When ready to assemble the dessert, whip and sweeten sufficient cream for both filling and topping. Carefully cut the wedges you have marked. Slice each wedge into two layers, placing the lower layer on the plate and keeping the upper layer adjacent to the plate. Spread butter on the open face of the lower layer of shortcake. Divide strawberries to ensure fair shares! Using half of your strawberries, put some on each buttered wedge. Then add a generous dollop of whipped cream. The tricky part is getting the top piece on the wobbly

Nickie with a sampling of wild strawberries.

strawberry/whipping cream-covered lower layer without breaking it. It can be done. Finally slather whipping cream on top of the dessert and ladle the remaining strawberries on top of the whipping cream for the prettiest effect. Alternatively, you can assemble one large shortcake—and while this is certainly easier to assemble, it's much harder to serve neatly. Another option is to make individual shortcakes.

Although we did pick commercial strawberries, the best berries were found wild on our own fields. Raspberry-picking was definitely a job for the strong-of-heart. The brambles, the scratches and the mosquitoes still deter me. But Andrew, with his extraordinary ability to ignore discomfort, still sets out, armed with bucket, thick boots, sturdy denim jeans and a broad-brimmed hat, returning always with sufficient for our dessert. Nick and Nigel, ardent berry-pickers both, were equally intrepid.

After strawberries and raspberries, all that was left to do in the berry mode was to pick currants. We had inherited a red currant bush from the Millers. Red currants are exorbitantly priced in the stores, so we cherished the fruit, using it to make a Dutch dessert in which equal quantities of raspberries and red currants are macerated for several hours at room temperature in sugar—yielding an intensity of colour and flavour without equal. However, when our forestry consultant told us red currant bushes harboured a virus fatal for our newly planted white pine, we brutally uprooted it.

In place of the red currant bush, we planted a black currant bush. Very soon, it was so prolific that we became desperate for recipes. Black currants are too tart to be eaten straight off the bush. One option was to make pear and black currant pies, but most of our black currants became jam. Later we learned black currant bushes were just as bad as red currant bushes for transmitting disease to pines.

Black Currant and Rhubarb Jam

Simmer 1 lb rhubarb cut in 1-inch pieces with 2 lbs washed black currants in 15 oz water for 30-40 minutes. Add 3 lbs sugar and stir over a low heat until dissolved. Then cook rapidly for 15-20 minutes, stirring enough to prevent burning. To test whether jam is done, I put a drop or two on a saucer and place the saucer in the freezer to enhance cooling. A jelly-like consistency indicates jam is sufficiently cooked. The jam should be removed from the heat while this testing procedure is carried out.

The following instructions for bottling are from *More Put a Lid on It! Small-Batch Preserving Year Round* (E. Topp & M. Howard, Macmillan Canada, 1999). After boiling mason jars in water for 10 minutes and snap lids for 5 minutes, remove jars from water and fill with jam to within 1/2 inch of rim. Place snap lid on jar and apply screwband finger tight. Place jars in canner with sufficient water to cover jars by one inch. Bring to boil and heat for 5 minutes. Remove jars from canner. Cool for 24 hours. Check that lids have snapped downward and are concave. Tighten screwbands.

SUMMER HARVEST includes more than berries. Andrew's garden used to be generous in its yield of vegetables. A real treat was always our sensationally sweet green peas, although there are never enough of them. Then he started growing snow peas and mange-tout and they were great too. Peas must be very hardy, because Andrew can plant peas in the garden as early as March.

For some unexplained reason, our friendly fauna—groundhogs, raccoons and rabbits—initially paid no attention to standard, garden-variety green beans. These were so prolific that, even though delicious, they almost became a burden. A long time ago, the sight of green beans in our garden was enough to make a three-year-old visitor from downtown Toronto ecstatic. She hadn't ever seen food growing in a garden. That the beans she had seen in the grocery store came from a garden astonished and delighted her. How many hours have we spent since then, Nickie and I, picking, washing, blanching and freezing green beans! When French-style bean seeds became available, a whole new bean-experience began. These beans are extremely thin, only a fraction of the diameter of ordinary green beans. They are delectable beyond description. We never could have too many of them.

The fauna also allowed us to harvest cherry, plum and beefsteak tomatoes, asparagus, green and red peppers, leeks, onions, potatoes, eggplant, Jerusalem artichokes and broccoli. Cherries are a different story. In spite of our best efforts, including dangling foil pie plates from the branches and even vain (and costly) attempts to cover the tree with netting, the birds have always eaten all our cherries before they are ripe enough to pick.

Luckily most of the flowers don't get eaten. As summer progresses, climbing red roses are set off like jewels against the dark barn siding, while in the garden, phlox, lilies, delphiniums, lupins and gladioli bring joy to the beholder. However, the most spectacular display is always the richly purple clematis that clings to and spreads over the stone walls surrounding the kitchen patio door. Beneath it, a dense bed of violet lavender fills the air with its sweet scent.

***

NOT SURPRISINGLY, water conservation is a major concern during the summer. The well can run dry and has on several occasions, usually in mid-August after a prolonged drought. The summer of 1999 saw many farmers' wells running dry—a catastrophe for livestock and crops. Of course it doesn't help that the current Ontario government permits commercial water bottlers to withdraw millions of gallons of groundwater in Grey County. With great fanfare, just prior to the last election, they imposed a province-wide moratorium on new licences for withdrawing water. As soon as they were voted back into power, licences were granted to take water for bottling in Grey County. Whatever the reason for depleted water supplies, we and our guests routinely conserve water all year long.

Water is precious and we never forget. We turn the tap off while brushing our teeth. Washing dishes under a running kitchen tap is discouraged—dishes get washed only in a dishpan, and hot rinse water is used to augment the soapy water. After we wash salad, vegetables and fruit, the water is carefully carried to the garden for favourite flowers and bushes. Even water used for cooking vegetables gets taken to the garden after it cools down. A house full of people means that toilets are kept busy, so with the help of our son-in-law Michael, we installed low-volume toilets long before they were generally available. To help us further, Andrew's uncle, Kim Krenz made signs to put up in the bathrooms:

If it's yellow, let it mellow!
If it's brown, flush it down!

One thing always leads to another. Conserving water goes hand in hand with collecting compost. Not only is compost good for the garden where it helps retain moisture and makes pulling up weeds much easier, but also, in the days when we had to take everything in knapsacks back to the car on skis, any way by which we could reduce our load of garbage was very welcome.

Ecological virtue is all very well, but it's hardly fun.

⟨✦⟩

FOR FUN WE WENT to the Bognor Barbecue. It's been a mid-July event for the past 30 years. The venue is the Bognor Hall built in 1957 and officially opened in May 1958. The hall on its own is devoid of any esthetic appeal. A squat rectangle built of cement blocks, unadorned by any attempt at landscaping, it could easily be mistaken for a small factory or warehouse. Yet the program for the opening ceremonies shows how much the hall represented the generosity and the effort of the whole community. The volunteerism was extraordinary—3,218 hours of donated labour. The hall became the centre of much of the social life of the community. Showers, dances, bingos, craft shows, Women's Institute meetings and the Bognor Barbecue all took place there. In preparation for the barbecue, families of hall board members canvassed neighbours to sell advance tickets. It was wise to buy tickets early because by the day of the event, they were often sold out. Those living close to Bognor were always asked (and still are) to contribute some food, usually pies or salads. I always made two lemon meringue pies although I found it amazing that there were actually people who preferred them to fresh berry pies.

By the day of the barbecue, borrowed picnic benches were set up in the dusty parking lot. The truck from Kitchener would roll up, park close to the Hall, and unload and fire up the long, rectangular barbecue. Vast quantities of pink, lean, and oh-so-tender smoked pork chops waited in cardboard boxes to be grilled. By 4:00 p.m. a lineup started to form outside the main entrance to the hall and at 5:00 p.m. the doors opened. Just inside, volunteers manned a desk and ticked off the numbers on the proffered tickets. The line snaked into the main room: a stage at the far end, the floor polished for dancing, curtains hanging limply from the windows. The hall became increasingly hot as it filled with people and the afternoon sun shone fiercely through the windows. Hundreds of people came from far and near. Conversation helped shorten the wait, which could be as long as one hour for those foolish enough to arrive as late as 5:30 or 6:00 p.m. The pork chops were grilled as needed. They could not be rushed or cooked in advance.

Eventually the lineup would bring us to the door at the far corner of the hall leading to the back stairs. At the first landing, there is a door out to the parking lot. During events such as Saturday night dances when the Hall was still dry, men in search of masculine conversation and liquid refreshment could exit by this door. They would stand between parked cars in the dark and enjoy the contents of their bring-your-own mickies. But at the barbecue, in broad daylight, that didn't happen. Going on down to the foot of the stairs, you entered the basement. It has a superbly equipped, commercial-style kitchen, separated by a counter from a large dining area. The dining area can seat about 200 at the same time, at long board tables with metal legs and noisy chairs. Men on the hall board with large enamel teapots walked up and down the aisles between tables, pouring tea for those who had already begun eating.

The moment you were in the basement, you were handed a paper plate with a pork chop on it. You did not select your chop. That was the responsibility of two men who dispensed them. I always suspected that larger chops were given to men—most disappointing for tall women like me with large appetites. While men doled out the meat, ladies were definitely in charge of all the other food. A team in the kitchen had to work hard to keep replenishing the large bowls of mashed potato salad, jellied salads, three-bean salad and cole slaw. The salads were amplified by bread, pickles and relishes. Farmers work long hours in the summer. The buffet serving dishes emptied quickly, proving a local saying: hunger makes a good sauce.

With plate heaped high, the diner had to decide where to sit down and eat—in the basement which was cool and noisy, or outside in the hot and dusty parking lot swarming with horseflies. For people like me who lusted for pies, there was a strategic advantage to staying in the basement, because that was where the pies were. Not in the kitchen, but at the other end of the basement, protected and distributed by a separate contingent of ladies. Those for whom pies were the major attraction, inevitably made at least one exploratory foray to the pie tables during the long wait upstairs. You'd descend by the front stairs, carefully survey the pies and wonder, would the pies you really wanted to eat still be there by the time it was your turn to come down the back stairs to eat? Sometimes there'd be a second foray 30 minutes later to assess how many pies had been eaten in the interval. You might be tempted to ask a friendly face to reserve a pie until you got there, if it were a particular favourite. That ploy sometimes worked.

Unfortunately, before you could begin on the pies, you had to eat your chop and salads. There would be some pies already on the table, and the pie ladies would always come with more. What a choice! Let me count the kinds: apple, blueberry, strawberry, rhubarb, red currant, strawberry and rhubarb, rhubarb custard, peach, sour cream, raisin, butterscotch, coconut cream, chocolate cream, banana cream and lemon meringue. At a minimum, taking it slowly, we could usually sample three kinds of pies and with sufficient discretion, avoid looking too greedy. Andrew and I, by sharing our three selections, were able to sample up to six kinds each. In the seventies, both our eyes and our stomachs were much larger than they are now. The berry pies always went first but even at the end of the evening, there would be other kinds of pie left. There'd also be extra pork chops, frozen, and we usually bought a package to take home.

IT WAS BECAUSE of the Bognor Barbecue that we decided we had to get the recipe for sour cream pie from Mildred Carmichael. Along the way, she introduced us to a new expression, namely "a skinny pie." A skinny pie was something no self-respecting cook would ever dare serve. Good cooks make generously filled pies and that is what Mildred certainly did.

Until we lived in Bognor, we had never encountered anything like this sour cream pie. Claimed to be unique to the immediate area—Walter's Falls, Bognor, Strathaven, Massey and the Beaver Valley—this pie used up cream that had soured in the days when everyone had their own milk cow and no one had a refrigerator. We loved it. However, those who don't like raisins should skip this recipe. It's a variation on a raisin pie—but what a splendid variation!

Mildred Carmichael's Sour Cream Pie

Have prepared a baked 9-inch pie shell. (See previous chapter for Hougues Magues pastry recipe.) In heavy saucepan, simmer together until caramelly and thickened 1 cup each of sour cream, raisins and brown sugar. Beat 2 egg yolks. Add 2 tbsp flour and mix. Add 1 cup milk, 1/4 tsp baking soda, 1/4 tsp salt, and 1/2 tsp cinnamon. While stirring, pour hot mixture gradually into the egg mixture. (This prevents eggs from cooking too quickly and making lumps.) When completely combined, return to saucepan and cook until thick, being careful not to burn or boil. Some recommend that to get the best results, this is the point at which the baking soda should be added, not in the previous step. Let mixture cool and pour into pie shell. Cover top with meringue made by beating 2 leftover egg whites until stiff and then beating in 1 tbsp sugar. Bake at 375°F until meringue is golden. *Or* use 2 whole eggs instead of egg yolks, and garnish pie with whipped cream. Another alternative is to use baked tart shells for individual serving, but I prefer this recipe as a pie.

Another highlight of the Bognor Barbecue was the jellied salads. To ignore jellied salads would be unforgivable. Gastronomic snobs predictably disdain them. In their eyes, to eat a sweet jellied salad with a main course is just unthinkable. However, anyone who is prepared to eat applesauce with pork, cranberry sauce with turkey, or pineapple-glazed ham should be willing at least to try one jellied salad.

Pineapple Carrot Jellied Salad

Thoroughly drain a 19 fluid oz (540 mL) can of crushed pineapple (not tidbits, and not chunks), reserving 1 cup of juice. Measure 1 cup of fruit. Dissolve one 6 oz orange jelly powder with 1 cup boiling water and add 1 cup juice. Stir in fruit, 1 1/2 cups grated carrots and 1/2 cup chopped nuts. Chill in 1 1/2 quart mould until set. When ready to serve, remove jellied salad from mould by running cold water over outside surface of mould. Place a serving plate upside-down on top of the mould and flip plate and mould over so that the salad settles on the plate.

Orange and Lemon Layered Fruit Mold

Drain a 19 fluid oz can of fruit cocktail and keep the juice. Add enough water to juice to make 1 3/4 cup. Heat 1 cup of juice to boiling. Pour into bowl with 3 oz orange jelly powder. Dissolve powder and add remaining liquid. Pour into 1 1/2 quart mould and chill until set. Dissolve 3 oz lemon jelly powder in 1 cup of boiling water. Add 2 tbsp lemon juice. When cool, blend in 1 cup mayonnaise. Chill until partially set and then stir in drained fruit. Pour over orange layer. Chill until set. Unmould to serve as described above.

Cheese and Pineapple Jellied Salad

Drain a 19 fluid oz can of crushed pineapple, reserving juice. Dissolve 6 oz orange jelly powder in 1 cup boiling water.

Add 1 cup of juice. When cool, add 3/4 cup mayonnaise, then
chill in 1 1/2 quart mould until partly set. Add 1 cup drained
fruit, 1 cup cottage cheese, 1 tbsp minced onion, 1 cup chopped
celery and stir. Chill until set. Unmould when ready to serve.

***

VOLUNTEER GROUPS in small communities all across Ontario
continue to put on events similar to the Bognor Barbecue to raise
money for worthwhile causes. Fish fries, beef and chicken barbecues,
turkey suppers, strawberry festivals—not invariably, but usually—offer
samplings of rural Ontario's favourite foods. Even now, well-done beef,
dryish roast turkey with bread stuffing, mashed potatoes, tinned vegetables, jellied salads, cole slaw and white bread remain staples. But as
more and more people choose to leave large urban centres to establish
themselves in small Ontario towns, changes in eating habits are occurring. Cappuccino is now sold in Owen Sound shopping malls, and
prosciutto, lobster tails and Arctic char can be found in the large supermarkets. Much as we enjoy the wider range of food items now available, it would be regrettable to forget the gustatory highlights of a previous era. So try making a sour cream pie or a jellied salad!

***

OBVIOUSLY THERE ARE pleasures to summer other than food.
Our pond for one thing. Early in the seventies, assisted by a grant
from the Ontario government, we fulfilled our dream and made a
rather large comma-shaped pond by widening a naturally occurring
ravine. We hired a bulldozer to construct the dam and installed an
elaborate overflow system, all meeting precise government specifica-
tions. With great foresight, Andrew instructed the high-hoe to place
a huge, flat-topped boulder near the top of the dam for swimmers to
dive off. After the fourteen-foot-high dam had been completed and

after the bulldozer had spread the excavated dirt evenly around the margins of the pond-to-be, we waited for nature to fill the muddy void with water. The pond filled much more quickly than we expected. A steady supply of water came from the creek and the flow increased whenever it rained. Natural springs pumped their ultra-cold water into the pond from the sides and from below. Before we knew it, the pond was full and water was dribbling over the upper margins of the outflow pipe.

However, the pond was far from beautiful. It was surrounded by a wide border—50-75 feet—of relentlessly bare sun-baked clay. Andrew planted pine trees and put in grasses, bull-rushes and water lilies at the edge of the pond. All have prospered in spite of unremitting assaults by beavers.

What could justify a government grant paying part of the costs for our pond? First, a large water reservoir was established. Secondly, the improved wildlife habitat was quickly occupied by deer, fox, coyotes, geese, ducks, blue herons, large and intimidating turtles and, of course, beavers. On the downstream side of the dam, we had a reliable watering hole for cattle, even during droughts. Our good fortune was that we ended up with a beautiful, secluded pond. The swimming was wonderful and the children could take short and safe journeys in a canoe.

Summer after summer in the mid-seventies, we would all pile into a derelict pickup truck owned by friends who were now renting the old Morrison farm. The distance from the Hougues Magues to the big pond is a 10-15 minute walk. Getting there is no problem, but on a hot summer day, getting back to the house is all uphill. So we were grateful for the ride. Folding chairs, towels, drinks and toys were brought along and we would sit on the dam, dive, jump or gingerly lower ourselves from the rock, swim and enjoy the sun. A truckload of sand had been brought in, so for a few years before it all washed away, the children could play in the sand. They could even set off for distant places in the red-sailed dinghy, just as Andrew had done many years ago on Caledon Lake.

**Cornelia and Andrew enjoy a lazy afternoon
by the big pond–before the beavers came.**

Such expeditions no longer occur, even though our Toyota 4-Runner could easily drive us overland to the big pond. All because of the beavers. The beavers have claimed territorial rights and are definitely in control. In the summer they eat wild apples and in the fall they fell trees. They have gnawed down many of the trees we planted—pines and willows—to build their hive-like houses (undermining our trails in the process) and to create new dams upstream. Annoyingly, the larger part of any tree they bring down remains unused and uneaten. In spite of one neighbour's disapproval (a weekend farmer like us, he writes a column for Canada's national newspaper and there revealed his inexplicable and provoking tolerance of beavers, although he may recently have changed his opinion), each year we invite a licensed trapper, Ben Redman, to trap our beaver. In fact, as I write, he has just left the pond having set three traps, placing them on the path the beavers take to get to the apple trees in the field. But each year, the beavers return. Their dams raise the water level upstream, so the trees they don't fell, they drown. The result is too many dead trees. Ben commented that the "people who don't want beaver to be trapped are always people who don't have any." That is precisely what we have noticed too.

Ben proves that the give-and-take philosophy Dick Murdoch described still exists. Dick had said "of course I didn't charge for taking store items to people on my mail route, because you knew you could count on them when you needed help." Ben knows how to cut down trees safely. Andrew fells trees all the time, but he was reluctant to tackle trees whose branches touched the Hydro line. So Andrew asked Ben (who used to work for Ontario Hydro, recently renamed Ontario Power Generation) for help. Ben and his son came and cut down six huge poplars. They encouraged us to sell them, not just burn them up. After the job was done and we'd talked over a cup of coffee, they refused Andrew's offer of payment. Why? "Because we can hunt and trap on your land." We needed their help and they gave it to us.

The beavers' worst legacy is "Beaver Fever." Whether they are around or not, the beavers have contaminated the big pond. Swimmers risk getting beaver fever, a protozoan diarrhea due to Giardia lamblia. We are not prepared to risk getting it even though it is treatable, although we know people who happily swim in beaver-infested ponds and remain unaffected. So now the pond primarily benefits wildlife. When we go down to the pond several times each summer for a tranquil meditation in the canoe, we often disturb a blue heron who resides there. It's quite a sight to see this large bird awkwardly rising from the edge of the pond and then majestically flying off.

Although the "big pond" was designed by the ministry, the plan they made in the early seventies would never be used today. First, ponds can no longer be constructed by widening and damming creek beds. Secondly, the overflow cannot be drawn from the surface of the pond. Surface water is always warmer so that when it runs off, the water temperature downstream is raised, disturbing the micro-environment. To prevent this from happening, intakes for overflows are better placed at the bottom of a pond.

THE NORTHERN LIGHTS: totally beyond our control and totally unpredictable. For no good reason, I associate them with August, although they occur in winter as well. They are always amazing and awe-inspiring. Unsuspectingly on your way from here to there, you look up and find the sky transformed by the mysterious and quivering aurora borealis. Immediately, every one in the house is called to come out—and neighbours are phoned in case they have not noticed. In the northern sky, flashing sheets of shimmering, cold, green rays pierce upward into the cupola of the universe. They sing. They fade. They disappear and then suddenly return. But too soon they die and are gone. Mortals are engulfed with wonder.

More constantly, the night skies of summer encourage stargazing. With blankets and sweaters to hold off the chill of dewy August nights, we sit on lawn chairs and identify in the black sky whole galaxies, stars, planets and satellites—and count shooting stars.

Chapter 9

Autumn Rituals

Chopping is now about to commence,
and in this I feel very much interested,
as a supply of firewood is of the utmost importance.

Letter from Anne Langton, December 11, 1837.

I LOVE FALL, but it's always upon us too quickly. Increasingly early nightfalls in August remind us September is coming and by my calendar, fall begins on September 1, not September 21. Another sign that fall is imminent is the arrival of cluster flies in the house. Cluster flies are a rural, not an urban problem, for which all city dwellers should be grateful. They are members of the fly order Diptera and resemble house-flies. Cluster flies are distinguished by their sluggish behaviour, yellow thoracic hairs and wings that overlap at rest. House-flies do not overlap their wings. No physical barrier can keep them out of any farmhouse. They could not even be kept out of the new hospital when it first opened on the outskirts of Owen Sound some years ago. Cluster flies peak in the early fall and again in early spring. They are countless in number. They spot the windows and blacken the windowsills. They cluster by the hundreds and die and then more cluster and more die. In the evening, in a frenzy, they dive-bomb light bulbs and bat away inside lampshades.

After a week away from the farm, we would find flies piled up on the windowsills and floors to such an extent that the only way to get rid of them was to sweep them up by the dustpanful, or to vacuum them. The trouble with vacuuming was that the heat of the motor roasted them, releasing a horrible musty smell the moment the vacuum was turned on. Distasteful as it was, there was and is only one thing to do, and that is clean them up as quickly as possible. As soon as we arrived Friday evenings, Andrew would vacuum (he was tall enough to be able to vacuum flies clinging to the ceiling) while I unpacked the food and clean laundry. Guests from the city found it hard to conceal their revulsion, but they gamely tried.

Our first attempt to control cluster flies was ecologically correct, inexpensive and futile. We bought a system, guaranteed to work, at the Keady Farmers' Market. Among the 200 or more vendors who attend this market just to the south and east of Owen Sound every Tuesday morning, was a retired farmer who had devised a system for catching cluster flies. He sold us a large pickle jar into which, after half-filling it with water, we were supposed to drop a piece of fresh fish. The pickle jar lid was adapted so that flies attracted by the smell of rotting fish could get into the jar, but not out of it. Placed in the garden, smelling of fish and with a thick floating layer of drowned fly carcasses, the jars purportedly would esthetically offend no one. This ingenious method didn't work. It did trap some flies but had no noticeable impact on the overall population.

Happily, cluster flies are no longer as much of a problem at the Hougues Magues. After 25 years of putting up with cluster flies, we are largely rid of them. Every fall and spring, the exterior of the house and the attic get sprayed with extended-action Permethrim, based on a chrysanthemum-derived pyrethroid. The cluster fly problem is reduced, but for how long? Will the flies develop resistance to Permethrim?

There is one other autumn nuisance that must be faced. Field mice like to return to the warmth of the house as the weather gets colder. Mice are just a fact of life and they will live in the Hougues Magues longer than I ever will. We can't get rid of them, but we do try to keep their numbers down. A cat would be ideal, but I am allergic to cats. Traps were inadequate to the job and repugnant to empty and reset. Another route was Warfarin, but mice develop resistance to Warfarin. Instead, we feed them a bromide product. Occasionally the mice take revenge, dying hidden in the house, often behind the stove, and for a day or two there is an unmistakable odour. Luckily desiccation occurs quickly. The odour is a trivial problem compared to having mouse droppings in the kitchen drawers. We just have to remember to remove the bromide bait when dogs come to visit.

But fall in Sydenham offers much more than invasions of cluster flies and field mice.

FALL PROMISES, and usually delivers, beautiful, clear, crisp weather. By October, it swathes the landscape in golds and crimsons, a glorious performance by deciduous trees. Before dropping their leaves for winter, trees erupt in ecstatic colour, transforming both rural hills and city streets and gardens.

In fall we must also finish dealing with summer's bounty. Kitchen work is unavoidable. Prune plums are purchased at the market and taken home to be halved, freed of their pits, and laid out on cookie sheets for freezing. Their fate is to be used throughout the year to make plum cakes, always a favourite dessert both in Toronto and at the farm.

Barbara Haber's Plum Cake

The recipe that follows is for one cake. I always quadruple the recipe and make four cakes: small (6 inches), medium, large and very large. Usually I freeze all four cakes, placing each one in a plastic bag closed with a twist after sucking out the air. When I need a dessert which can serve as few as four, or as many as 10 guests, I take out the appropriate sized cake and put it frozen in a 325°F oven for about 15 to 25 minutes depending on its size. The cake should be sprinkled with icing sugar using a spoon to push the sugar through a fine sieve and served barely warm. It can be eaten plain, with whipped cream or with ice cream. We like it best with whipped cream.

> Grease a 9-inch springform pan and heat oven to 350°F. Cream together 1/2 cup of unsalted butter and 3/4 cup white sugar until very well blended. Add 2 eggs, one at a time, beating with an electric mixer for at least five minutes. The mixture should become a very pale yellow with beating. Measure 1 cup sifted unbleached all-purpose flour. Return to sifter with 1 tsp baking powder and sift into egg mixture. Use the mixer as briefly as possible at the slowest speed, to mix in the flour. Then pour batter into springform pan. Take prune plum halves from freezer and place frozen on top of the batter until it is entirely covered with a single layer of plums. Drizzle 1 tbsp lemon juice over the plums. Sprinkle 1 tbsp sugar over the plums. Then, using a small sieve and spoon, sprinkle 1 tsp cinnamon over the plums. Bake for about 1 hour or until a sharp knife inserted in the middle comes out clean.

When necessary, I have made this cake with salted butter and regular all-purpose flour. The cake will still be good, but it will lack the nutty texture that results when the recipe is strictly followed.

While we are loyal customers at the Owen Sound Farmers' Market, using produce from our own garden is very satisfying. Usually by mid-September there is a good supply of green tomatoes in Andrew's garden that will never ripen. Because they are green does not mean they cannot be harvested. They fry up, especially when covered with flavoured crumbs, much better than ripe tomatoes do. But most of our green tomatoes are used for relish.

Hougues Magues Green Tomato Relish

This is a very simple recipe. It makes a superb relish for hot dogs, hamburgers, chicken, turkey or ham. If put in pretty bottles with an attractive label, the relish makes a nice hostess gift. The major challenge is to cook it until it is thick enough and not all watery. In the last 30 or 45 minutes of cooking time, it has to be stirred very frequently to prevent burning on the bottom. More than once I have been obliged to empty the half-cooked relish from one saucepan into another. Cleaning burned saucepans is something I'd rather not do.

> Chop 8 lbs of green tomatoes and put in large saucepan.
> Add 4 lbs brown sugar and 1 quart vinegar. Bring to a boil
> and then simmer for 3 hours. Add 1 tsp each of ground mace,
> cinnamon and cloves and boil another 15 minutes. Put in sterile
> jars and follow instructions given for Black Currant and Rhubarb
> Jam on page 89.

The garden also yields Jerusalem artichokes—a truly low-maintenance and reliable crop. They can be eaten in many ways, but are particularly good for a nice warm soup as days become cooler.

Andrew's Jerusalem Artichoke Soup

> Clean three slender leeks (1 inch in diameter) and cut
> in 1-inch pieces. Put in small saucepan with one small chopped
> onion and barely cover with water. Simmer 10 minutes or
> until just tender. Peel and coarsely chop sufficient Jerusalem
> artichokes to achieve a volume of about 3 cups. Put in large
> saucepan and add 3 cups milk. Simmer until tender which may
> take 45 min. Combine contents of two saucepans using hand-
> held blender to thoroughly mix. Add salt to taste. Sprinkle with
> chopped fresh chervil when serving.

Another fall task is to bring in the large golden onions whose green tops were stamped down to wither in the garden earlier in the summer. The onions are laid out on newspaper in the barn to continue drying. Andrew digs up any potatoes that haven't already been eaten—he firmly believes that potatoes taste best if cooked within minutes of being picked. There are never enough leeks.

<hr />

THANKSGIVING in Canada always occurs the second Monday in October, our last holiday weekend before Christmas. It's a time when the weather is still gentle, so gentle we often can still eat outdoors. The harvest is at its peak as are the fall colours. Almost always the whole family is at the Hougues Magues. That means our daughter Nicole is there with her husband Michael, their children Monique and Andrew, and Michael's mother Maria Martin. When Nigel and his wife Caroline lived in Montreal, they would also come, undeterred by the eight-hour drive.

The Thanksgiving menu is largely, but not totally, predictable: roast turkey with a buttery bread and onion stuffing, cranberry sauce, yam casserole, roast potatoes, a green vegetable, a tossed green salad (salad is always eaten after the main course in our house) and pumpkin pie with whipped cream. It goes without saying, there is always wine during and coffee after the meal. Maria, a splendid cook, can be counted on to bring an interesting hors d'oeuvre, different every time she comes. We work hard outside, come in with huge appetites, eat too much and sleep well.

Yam Casserole

I have never paid attention to the difference between sweet potatoes and yams. I just buy large ones, and sometimes they are labelled sweet potatoes and sometimes not. We first enjoyed this casserole when we were living in North Carolina, and I have made it for Thanksgiving ever since. I never refer to a recipe—it just happens as follows. How much liquid you add will be determined by the volume of puréed sweet potatoes. How much flavouring you add is a personal choice. This casserole can be made the day before.

Simmer three large yams in water until tender. Peel.
Purée in blender. Add about 1/4 cup soft butter, 1/2 tsp salt,
1/3 cup brown sugar, 1 tbsp orange zest, 1/4 to 1/2 cup of
orange juice, 2 to 3 tbsp sherry, and cinnamon and nutmeg
to taste. Mix thoroughly. Put in greased casserole. Bake at
325°F for 45 minutes or until hot enough to serve.

As for pumpkin pie, I have tried dozens of recipes and never
been really satisfied. So I've made my own, which may work for you.

Thanksgiving Pumpkin Pie

Prepare one 9-inch pie crust with Hougues Magues pastry
and partially bake as follows:

Line crust with aluminum foil and fill with raw rice or beans to
add weight. Bake at 350°F for 15 minutes. Measure about
2 cups of canned pumpkin purée and place in large bowl. Beat
in 2 eggs, 3/4 cup brown sugar, 1 cup cream or milk or
condensed milk, and 1/2 tsp each ground mace, cloves, cinnamon and nutmeg. Fill the partially baked pie crust and bake at
350°F for 1 hour or until inserted knife comes out clean. If a crack
appears on the surface of the filling, it is cooked. Serve at room
temperature with whipped cream.

BURNING FELLED TREES is our outside work on many fall weekends. In the seventies, no one could be oblivious to what had happened and was happening to Ontario's elm trees. In 1971, what we
were facing was a disaster which would eventually destroy more than
200 mature elm trees on our property, elms that would have to be cut
down and burned. To help achieve disease control and control the haz-
ard of falling branches, the Ontario government sponsored a program

that paid farmers $5.00 per tree up to a maximum of 100 elms if they were able to show they had felled and disposed of all the dead trees. We would collect that money, although we disposed of far more than 100 trees, working over several years. It is a tribute to the capacity of species to overcome adversity that elm trees continue to grow in Ontario although they usually die before reaching full maturity. Will they ever develop resistance to Dutch elm disease? In the 21st century, will their signature shape be restored to the Ontario landscape?

Even though the elms have long since been dealt with, there is always tree debris to burn every fall. Burning large volumes of debris efficiently—everything from coniferous branches which flame up instantly, to large logs which need to be coaxed into igniting—requires skill. An expert taught us how to construct and tend bonfires. The expert, Janos Hrabovszky, learned how to burn brush in Australia where he had emigrated from Hungary in the late 40s. We met him in the summer of '58 when he was a farm manager on an estate near Orangeville. We were living at the Caledon Lake cottage while Andrew, still a medical student, was a summer intern at the Orangeville hospital. Janos had driven a Volkswagen into a train and was brought to Emergency covered in blood and manure, reeking of gasoline and expostulating incoherently in Hungarian. While he recuperated in hospital, Andrew found him reading a book on antiques. In such strange ways do friendships begin.

Janos and his wife Lou later moved to Guelph in Ontario, Ithaca in New York State, and then New Delhi, Rome and Vienna. In spite of all those perambulations, Lou and Janos have been regular visitors to the farm since our very first year. And so it was that when Eddy Morrison's farm was put up for sale next door, Janos and Lou bought it.

Janos is never bashful about pointing out that there are better ways to do whatever it is you are doing. Our fire building left much to be desired. You cannot effectively persuade high piles of wood and brush to ignite by setting a fire in a small corner at the bottom, nor for that matter, by setting a fire on top. Janos began with two large pieces of wood in parallel, using kindling in between to start the fire. Then as it got going, he began to feed the fire, pulling off branches as needed from the brush heap. Large pieces always go in the centre, parallel to the foundation of the fire. Smaller, but highly inflammable branches must be piled on sparingly, because otherwise the intense flames they generate starve the bottom of oxygen. That's how we did it, usually in the fall, but also in the winter and early spring. The barn debris and the elms are long since gone. Disposing of diseased trees and pruned branches is a task that will never end.

⁕

LATE FALL has many tasks. It's time to make and spread mulch. Mulch spread around trees and bushes begins to decompose over the winter and in the spring helps retain moisture in the soil. Weeding is also much easier.

Over spring and summer, a huge pile of branches accumulates behind the barn mainly from pruning trees in the garden, but also from pruning done in the forest close to the house. When the pile is sufficiently massive, Andrew rents a huge and noisy chipper with a gaping maw into which the branches are thrust and from which human hands must maintain a respectful distance. The huge pile of branches is rapidly converted into a relatively small pile of mulch, which, if we are lucky will last for the next year.

Late fall is also the time when Andrew wraps and ties burlap around favoured ornamental shrubbery. It seems paradoxical that the burlap is not meant to protect from the cold as much as it is meant to protect from a strong sun during a winter thaw. In recent years, it has also become necessary to shield yews, euonymus and rhododendrons with chicken wire or woven fence wire to protect them from hungry deer. Andrew also tidies up flowerbeds and puts outdoor furniture into storage. Then he attends to gas-driven motors which must be drained of fuel, batteries which must be brought inside the house,

The rented – and hazardous – woodchipper.

and the cistern pump and outdoor faucets which must be drained of water—a busy time.

Next is firewood. Our fireplace gives us warmth and pleasure. Fall is the time to check whether the supply of firewood in the barn will be sufficient over the winter. We have never needed to purchase firewood with all the trees we have on the farm. However, cutting the logs into suitably sized pieces and hauling them to the barn takes time. Everyone helps—even our grandson Andrew, when he was only six, would work for several hours loading firewood without flagging.

But there is still more for Andrew to do in preparation for winter. Nineteenth-century Ontario surveyors laid out lots so that in our area, 100-acre farms were just two fields wide. That meant each farm, including ours, was a narrow strip, going back a long way from the road. However, another 50 acres was tacked onto our northern boundary because the 100-acre strip immediately north of us was totally unsuitable for farming. Half was assigned to the neighbour on its far side, and half was assigned to our farm. The result is our 150 acres cover a sufficiently wide and topographically diverse area to provide scope for interesting cross-country ski trails designed by Andrew. Skiers can now circle the frozen pond, slide through the sun-dappled shelter of our woodlot, contemplate our babbling brook with its sculpted ice formations and coast down stretches of gently sloping fields. Skiers can also enjoy the excitement of long steep runs (if brave) or less challenging runs (if cautious).

Only Andrew will remember my ill temper when we were cross-country skiing during our first years at the farm. He would plunge cheerfully through the brush, ignoring branches and young saplings, totally unhindered by anything that stood in his way. I would follow up in the rear, skis entangled in the brush, cheeks smarting from whipping branches, sliding backwards while going uphill and unashamedly letting it be known that this was NOT FUN. All this has changed. With the help of friends over the years, trees have been removed to widen trails and branches pruned to clear them. Rough bridges have been laid over the creek. I now have good touring skis. And every fall, Andrew pushes his heavy brush mower up hill and down dale, often with the help of Nigel and young Andrew, getting rid of the undergrowth on the trails—so we can all enjoy clear skiing.

Of course, fall does not officially end until December 21. However, from early December on we are fully occupied with Christmas preparations and entertaining in Toronto. So on the last weekend we are at the Hougues Magues before Christmas, we always find time to decorate the house. Wreaths go on the doors, special candles are readied for lighting and garlands are draped over the mantels. Then when we return to the farm soon after Christmas, the right atmosphere welcomes us and we step into preparations for our wedding anniversary on December 28 and for New Year's Eve celebrations.

Fall races by.

Chapter 10

Winter Rituals

Mon pays, ce n'est pas un pays, c'est l'hiver.

Song by Gilles Vigneault, in a National Film Board of Canada film. 1965.

WE MIGHT WELL have chosen to spend Christmas routinely at the farm had it not been for my parents and Andrew's, who lived in Toronto and had no desire whatsoever to be at the farm in the wintertime. My mother was game to go anywhere any time, but my father, who had emigrated from Holland in 1927, had had his fill of rural Ontario winters in the thirties when he was a travelling salesman for McCormick's and Weston's biscuits. Andrew's parents usually spent Christmas with their daughter and her family. So we spent Christmas Eve with Andrew's parents at their home, and on Christmas Day my parents came to our Toronto home.

In retrospect, it's unbelievable that we did what we did. For several years, when the children were still young, we took down the Toronto Christmas tree on Boxing Day morning (December 26), packed the car with enormous quantities of food, plus wine, books, toys and anniversary presents, tied the tree on top, drove to the farm, and had finished redecorating the tree by late afternoon, having brought absolutely everything in on skis. Tirelessly, Andrew would make two or three trips back and forth from house to car. I never made more than one trip, although Nigel and Nickie often did.

One Christmas, Andrew and the children actually dragged in, over the snow, on a toboggan, a Victorian glass-fronted dresser about

113

7 feet tall. It came in two pieces, the top section with shelves and glass doors, and the bottom section with two drawers and two cupboards. It had been Andrew's Christmas present to me, and there was no way I wanted to wait until spring to enjoy it at the Hougues Magues. It arrived safely in two stages.

Much of the food we brought in was leftovers from our Christmas menus—leftover turkey, stuffing and vegetables and left-over Christmas pudding. And we always have a special jellied salad, quite different from the Bognor summer repertoire of sweet jellied salads. Our jellied salad is reserved for Christmas brunch and it is well complemented by ham, tongue, green salads and a Russian salad. The latter also finds its way to the Hougues Magues. On Christmas Eve I always make extras of both recipes so we can bring them to the farm to eat between Christmas and New Year's. The first recipe comes from Andrew's mother, who liked to be called Margie.

Margie's Christmas Salad

Heat 1 can undiluted tomato soup. Soak one 3 oz package lemon jelly powder in 1/2 cup cold water for 5 minutes. Stir into hot soup. Cream 8 oz cream cheese in blender and then add hot soup mixture. Blend just until the mixture is uniformly combined. When cool, add 1 1/2 cups chopped celery, 1 small diced onion, 1/2 cup chopped walnuts and 1 cup mayonnaise. Mix thoroughly. Put in serving bowl and refrigerate a day ahead or at least several hours before serving.

Hougues Magues Russian Salad

Put contents of 24 oz bag of frozen mixed vegetables—sometimes called "Macedoine"—into large pot of boiling water. There should be carrots, peas, green beans and corn in the mixture. As soon as the water returns to boiling, remove pan from heat and drain vegetables in large colander. Immediately put under tap to run cold water on the vegetables. Leave vegetables in colander to allow water to drain off and store covered in refrigerator until ready to serve. Hard boil 6 to 8 eggs. Store in refrigerator and peel and chop just before serving. When ready to serve, drain a 2 oz jar of capers and mix together with the cooked vegetables and prepared eggs. Add sufficient mayonnaise to bind vegetables. Sometimes I add 2 tsp curry powder. Mound salad on serving platter and decorate as desired with olives, or quarter sections of more eggs, or sliced tomatoes.

WE ALWAYS HAD a few days on our own before company arrived to celebrate the New Year. With or without company, daytime activities in the winter centred on cross-country skiing although the children preferred tobogganing. The pond would always freeze over but usually with a surface too rough for skating. Then there was visiting to do, or pruning, or making more bonfires. And always, reading.

The cross-country skiing made use of Andrew's splendid trails, but sometimes we would leave the trails and visit neighbours. Arriving so quietly on skis, we often surprised them. There was always more time for visiting in winter. One destination would be Ruth and Lloyd Carmichael's home, the farm where Lloyd's brother had been living when our farm endured the bankruptcy sale in the 1930s. Lloyd and Ruth have now sold the family farm and live in Owen Sound. At Christmas Ruth always baked a huge array of sweets. But first we would chat and admire the Christmas presents arranged neatly under the artificial tree. Most of our Bognor neighbours had artificial Christmas trees, probably because they don't make a mess.

After we'd talked to Ruth for a while, Lloyd would come in from the barn, taking off his duck-billed cap to reveal the pale skin of his forehead untouched by the sun, a real contrast to the rest of his face. We would be invited to the kitchen table, laid out with lace doilies and good china and Christmas napkins, and there we would drink hot tea and choose cookies and squares from among the many Ruth had prepared. A favourite in the Bognor area is:

Ruth Carmichael's Butterscotch Mallows

These are very popular but they are quite sweet.

Melt 2 cups butterscotch chips (alternatively, 1 cup butterscotch and 1 cup chocolate chips) with 1/2 cup butter. Cool. Add 1 cup peanut butter, 1/2 cup chopped nuts and one small package miniature marshmallows and mix. Pat gently into greased 9x13 inch pan. Cut into squares.

Ruth Carmichael's Mud Pies

The intriguing name of these cookies warrants making them at least once.

Bring to a boil in a saucepan: 2 cups white sugar, 1/2 cup milk, 1/2 cup shortening, 5 tbsp cocoa, 1 tsp vanilla, and 1/2 tsp salt. Remove from heat and cool. Add 3 cups quick Quaker Oats and 1 cup sweetened shredded or flaked coconut. Shape cookies to desired size, preferably small since they are sweet, and store.

Nick remembers with pleasure that these squares and more were served at the shower Ruth gave for her just before her 1980 wedding.

The one Sydenham recipe I have never asked for is a popular Christmas cake made with jujubes instead of candied fruits. We much prefer the Christmas cake I make every Halloween (October 31) using an extravagant recipe from Andrew's English grandfather. But it does not belong to the Hougues Magues because I never bake it there—we just eat it there.

WE ALSO SKIED UP to Norm and Frieda's and to their next door neighbours, Mel and Mabel Morrison. Mel regaled us with gossip about township governance, past and present. Having been on the township council, he knew at first hand what went on, admirable and otherwise. He told us stories about our house which he had visited as a young boy—how what was now the playroom above the kitchen used to be accessible only by the back kitchen stairs. Dan Morrison's sons as well as any hired help must have slept there, while Dan's daughters slept at the front of the house. Any young boys who, like Mel, were accompanying their parents to winter parties, were put to sleep there while the dancing went on below in our kitchen. There was no way that the boys could visit the girls, Mel told us.

He also told us that during one boisterous party, an oil lamp hanging from our kitchen ceiling crashed to the floor. And that our curving lane used to be the main north-south winter thoroughfare for the fifth line, when the horse-drawn cutters and sleighs detoured around the base of the hill rather than climb to the top and then descend again, just as Dick Murdoch described doing when he was delivering the mail. With some bitterness, Mel talked about how, as a young man, he had shovelled gravel to earn money—50 cents a day and all the whiskey you could drink.

Of all our neighbours, Mel was the one who most frequently visited us. He'd arrive unannounced, often at inconvenient times, and then he would begin talking and we would wonder if and when he would ever stop. But in spite of such thoughts, we always listened with interest and always wanted him to return. He was both challenging and entertaining.

Mel once tried to persuade me to run for township council, which was flattering but totally impossible for me to consider, given that I had to be in Toronto on weekdays. But it was interesting that he even made the suggestion. As an expert on roads (was this because of his labour in the gravel pits? Or because of his time on township council?), he declared that our lane was totally unsatisfactory. In Mel's opinion, our lane had been neither properly cambered nor gravelled. In fact, he had a very low opinion of the people who were in the gravel business, whom he thought took advantage of outsiders like us. So the next time we ordered gravel for the lane, Mel supervised, making sure that the grader made a proper downward slope from the centre of the lane to the edges, that the right kind of gravel was delivered, and that it would be properly spread. The fact that we couldn't afford the right kind of gravel was beside the point; instead of using the right kind of gravel for the whole lane, we would have to use it for the crucially important sections of the lane. Mel had standards, quite rigid standards, not only for lanes and roads, but also for the maintenance of barns which he considered to be of prime importance.

Mabel, Mel's wife, never came visiting. She was a cheery soul, so proud of her grandchildren and such an excellent housewife. When you visited Mabel, you didn't get sweets. She offered wholewheat muffins which were very satisfying to skiers coming in from the cold on a winter afternoon.

Mabel Morrison's Whole Wheat Muffins

Grease muffin pans, sufficient for 18 muffins, and heat oven to 375°F. Cream together 1/4 cup butter, 1/2 cup white sugar and 1/2 cup brown sugar. Sift together 1 sifted cup all-purpose flour, 1 sifted cup whole-wheat flour and 1 tsp baking powder. Mix 1 cup sour milk (you can sour the milk by adding 1 tsp vinegar) and 1/2 tsp baking soda. Mix 1/3 of the flour mixture into the sugar mixture, then 1/2 of the milk, another third of the flour, the remaining 1/2 of the milk and finally the remaining 1/3 of the flour, mixing well after each addition. Divide batter among 18 muffin tins. Bake for 20 minutes.

In Sydenham, people still have open caskets at funerals. After Mabel died, we went to the "visitation." My diary notes that Mabel was wearing her turquoise evening dress, the one she had worn to

Nickie's engagement party in Toronto in 1979. She also wore her spectacles. Mel's farm was sold soon after and he moved into a retirement home in Owen Sound. It was heartbreaking to visit Mel; without Mabel and without his farm, he was a broken man.

⁓✦⁓

OUR CROSS-COUNTRY SKIS gave us access to the forested areas off the ski trails. Our growing forest needed, and still needs, pruning. By the time a white pine stands 12 or more feet high, the lowest branches have died off for lack of sun and should be sawn off. By the time the tree is 30 feet high, it is advisable to prune off the branches as high as you can reach with a pruning saw, ultimately up to 14 feet from the ground, in order to maximize the quality of the stand. That has been a Sisyphean task—pruning, pruning and pruning, with not even the remotest possibility of ever completing all the pruning that could be done. Does this bother us? Not at all. We just enjoy spending several hours each weekend in the winter woods, clearing out one small section at a time, with me tackling the lower branches and Andrew the higher ones, often with friends and family helping. The risks are minimal. Getting sawdust in your eyes is almost inevitable unless you wear protective glasses and even then the occasional chip slips in. And at the end of the day, you know you've been working—shoulders ache from overhead pruning and hands may develop a few blisters. But you feel deliciously relaxed.

While we prune we are also inspecting the trees. We look for white blister rust which is a fungal disease spread from wild gooseberries and domestic currant bushes. What looks like white paint, dribbles down the trunk, and the curve of the trunk is flattened. When we find a tree that has been hit, Andrew fells it with his chainsaw and cuts it into manageable pieces that we can drag out to an open space to be burned as soon as possible. Some of our guests seem to enjoy tending bonfires in spite of the occasional singed eyebrow or choking fit when the wind, unexpectedly changing direction, thrusts smoke into lungs.

What we need to do, and haven't yet done, is send out a hunting party in the spring to locate and destroy the wild gooseberry bushes down by the creek.

⁂

WINTER EVENINGS ARE LONG. In January, darkness falls by 5:00 p.m., but it's never a problem to fill the evening hours—nice dinners, conversation, jigsaw puzzles, games, then time for bed. When we have no company, there's time for reading. No television. Our children did not seem to notice its absence when they were young, and our grandchildren have never complained.

Some Saturday evenings we'd put on our skis again (I've often skied in skirts, even long skirts) and head out to the car because there was a dance at the Bognor Hall. We would dance to country music played by local musicians and Norm McKibbon might call a few squares. Sometimes Alec Carmichael would do a clog dance with his daughter Gail, and afterwards glide around the floor with his wife Mildred. Mildred (of the sour cream pies) and Alec were both light on their feet and loved dancing, often going several times a week to dances in Walter's Falls or Owen Sound, even when they were in their late seventies. Mildred often sported battery-powered earrings. They were miniature stoplights that flashed red, amber and green, and were always a source of amusement.

At regular intervals, many of the men would leave the dance floor and return later smelling of rye whiskey. A few continued the teetotalling tradition that Dick Murdoch's grandparents had followed almost a century ago. In the meantime, the music would continue. These dances were attended by all generations, from infants and children to nonagenarians. Those not up to dancing would be seated on chairs pushed up against the walls all around the hall. Children would jump around on the dance floor, babies would be bounced on knees, and you could chat with people you'd not seen since the last dance.

Even when there was a special event at the hall, such as a "shower," the first part of the evening would be much the same. Showers were held for weddings, for farmers retiring and moving into Owen Sound, or to help a family who had lost their house in a fire. For a shower you would bring an envelope with a card and money and put it in a decorated box by the door. Back in the forties, when Elizabeth and John Gillies were married, 50 cents was what went in envelopes for their wedding shower.

What really distinguished a shower from a Saturday night dance were the personal tributes made to the couple being honoured. Special poems were written and read—and those poems would tell stories of the couple's life, long ago events which most in the hall knew all about. Sometimes the poetry evoked laughter, sometimes blushes. When Dick Murdoch retired from delivering the mail, Bob and Doreen Tuck wrote and sang a wonderful song in his honour, part of which follows.

> Along the Derry Dick would go
> Where the blustering winds do blow
> Through the sixth line with its boulders, oh so huge.
> Down the tricky town line hills
> To Queen's Valley wide and still,
> Then across the flat to conquer yonder ridge.
> For us folks on RR 1
> Yes – Dick's last delivery's done –
> Like the fifteen thousand times he did before.
> As we gather here today
> All us folks would like to say
> Thank-you Dick, how could we ever ask for more?

Later, the CBC would interview Dick and record the song. Now when Dick listens to the tape, his eyes get moist and he admits it "makes you lonesome for the people you knew."

Always at the end of evening events at about 11:30 p.m., "lunch" was served in the hall basement. Tea, white bread, sliced baloney, pickles, Cheez Whiz, homemade squares and sometimes a special cake were the standard offerings. It was pot-luck; everyone brought something. There were always many different kinds of squares. Below are two kinds we make at the Hougues Magues; the first is from Andrew's mother who must have made these brownies hundreds of times.

Margie's Brownies

Melt 1/2 cup butter and 2 squares bitter chocolate. Let cool. Mix two well-beaten eggs with 1 cup white sugar. Add alternately to egg mixture 1/2 cup all-purpose flour and the melted butter and chocolate. Bake at 350°F in a greased 8x8 inch pan for 15 minutes. Arrange 6-8 large marshmallows on top and bake for five minutes more. After cooling, chocolate icing (made with 1 cup icing sugar, 2 tbsp soft butter, 1 tbsp cream and 1 tbsp cocoa) can be put on top of the marshmallows. The marshmallows can be omitted.

Fabulous Lemon Squares

I'll take lemon squares over brownies any day. These lemon squares are to die for, as one of our friends says.

Combine in a food processor until mealy 1 cup soft butter, 1/2 cup icing sugar and 2 cups all-purpose flour. Pat dough into greased 9x13 inch pan, prick and bake at 350°F for 20 minutes. With electric mixer, combine 4 beaten eggs with 2 cups white sugar, 3 tbsp finely chopped lemon rind and 6 tbsp lemon juice. Pour egg mixture over the cooked dough. Bake another 15 minutes at 350°F or until set. Dust with icing sugar and cut into squares when cool.

After lunch was over at the hall, it was time to drive back to the Hougues Magues and ski down the lane. We always appreciated the fact that on a Saturday evening, unlike Fridays, we entered a warm house with warm beds.

Not surprisingly over thirty years, much has changed. Liquor can now be served in the Bognor Hall, and instead of the ring of chairs around the hall, tables are set up around the dance floor where people can put their drinks and sit with their friends. Such an arrangement doesn't encourage as much circulation. It also makes the dance floor smaller. Most of the "old-timers" we knew have died. The music and the faces have changed and so has the food. Instead of showers, there are Buck and Doe parties. Membership on the hall board has dwindled. But in July 1999, 700 people came to the Bognor Barbecue and there was no shortage of volunteers to serve the food.

<hr />

ANYONE LIVING IN CANADA who ignores the reality that winter is formidable is plain and simply foolish. Whether you live in Toronto (the same latitude as Rome and Northern California), or further north, winter is always waiting behind your back. If you're lucky, it's waiting only to remind you of your mortality. If you're unlucky, it's waiting to kill you. Winter's victims are the strong and the foolish, the weak and the wise. Winter's icy roads play with cars, spinning them into other cars, or hurling them overturned into ditches. Winter's whiteouts—heavy, swirling snow obscuring even the hood ornament on the car—leave drivers blindly helpless on highways. Whiteouts can even make a farmer lose his way going back to his own house from the barn.

Winter's cold wreaks its damage more subtly than do snow and ice, but it is just as threatening. Hypothermia strikes the solitary elderly in the "safety" of their homes, when their heating system fails and no one knows. It strikes young cross-country skiers like our son

Nigel and his friend Peter Ridgeway. Damp with sweat, they rapidly chill down and decide to lie in a comfortable snow bank to rest. By chance Andrew finds them and gets them both home quickly. It strikes Ted Milligan (one of the eight children with us our first night at the farm), lightly dressed because it is warm in the morning when he starts out on a 25 km snowshoe expedition with his schoolmates in Manitoba. A sudden 15°F temperature drop in the early afternoon, one broken harness, and deep, deep snow, result in Ted's being left behind while his friends seek help. He ends up in a hospital emergency room, comatose, to all purposes dead on arrival. Extraordinary efforts by the attending doctor, miraculously revived Ted. (For a while he was a news feature in the national media and even *Readers' Digest* had an article about his mishap.)

Most insidiously, winter oppresses the spirit. Seasonal affective disorder blights the life of those who suffer the feelings of depression triggered by long hours of darkness. It happens both in cities and in the country. Then there is cabin fever, when winter imprisons people, the frail and the elderly who cannot cope with snow and ice, the people like Mary Morrison who spent all winter, year after year, in her kitchen with its ever-present stench of urine. I remember the warmth of her smile, the dulling of her intellect, the subduing of her spirit. Winter didn't help.

The settlers who first came to Sydenham in the mid-19th century did not need to worry about the hazards of highways and motor vehicles. But they did have to worry about keeping warm and having enough stored food. One winter day, when the snow was swirling around the Hougues Magues, and the skies, when you could actually discern them, were low and leaden, and when no one in their right mind would have set foot outside other than for an emergency, I began reading *Reminiscences of North Sydenham* written in 1924 by Allan H. Ross. I was struck by the description of one James Gibson, born near Glasgow in 1805. He arrived in Toronto in 1841 where he "engaged in house building and general architecture." When he left Toronto in

1852 for Sydenham, he owned five houses in Toronto. He chose to set-tle on a farm about five miles northeast of Leith. According to Ross, so isolated was this farm that not until seven years after their arrival, did Mrs. Gibson see Owen Sound for the first time. Seven winters on an isolated farm! Ross reports that the community found Mr. Gibson to be "the finest type of Scottish gentleman of the old school. He had an urbanity and courtesy of manner that nothing seemed to disturb." What sort of life did they lead on that isolated farm? How did it rec-oncile with their memories of life in Glasgow and Toronto?

In many ways these settlers were less vulnerable to winter than we are at the beginning of the 21st century, dependent as we are on technology and fresh food. They had wood-stoves and adequate heat, a hand pump to provide water, coal oil lamps for light, cows to pro-vide milk, chickens to provide eggs, and foods such as salted pork and root vegetables that did not require refrigeration. They probably had a strong sense of confidence in their own ability to cope with all the physical rigours of winter.

WINTER HAS MANY FACES. It is so beguilingly benign when Sydenham skies sparkle blue, and the sun shines warmly on us as we sit on our south-facing patio, reading the weekend newspaper and drinking cappuccino—in February.

Chapter 11

Practising Frugality

But I can't give in as yet to eating sqirrells;
for they're for all the world, all as one as rats.

Letter XIV from Bridget Lacy, 1832
In *Authentic Letters from Upper Canada.*

I N THE EARLY SEVENTIES with two children in private schools, two mortgaged houses and only one wage earner, Andrew, who had just finished post-doctoral studies abroad in 1968, we had, as my mother used to say, to be "careful with our pennies." This led to very creative thinking. How otherwise could we renovate two houses simultaneously? Andrew and I recycled, refinished, dismantled, rebuilt, painted, wired, plumbed and repaired. I made clothes for the children, sometimes even using fabric from discarded clothes. I darned socks, lengthened and shortened hems as fashion required, patched jeans, turned collars and cuffs, and didn't send shirts out to be laundered, because my mother was always ready to help with the ironing. We tried to avoid buying anything we could make. I made our own breadcrumbs, mayonnaise, relishes, jams, salad dressing, granola and baked goods, rather than buying them ready-made. We rarely went to restaurants and never bought "fast foods." We were depression babies and knew how to be careful.

The Hougues Magues needed fittings, furniture and fixtures. What could we find around us? In Toronto people were forever putting perfectly good furniture out in their garbage. With consent from the householder, I was always ready to take home a chair or a side-table in need of gluing, or re-varnishing or re-upholstering. In the barn we found two chairs: a wooden rocking chair with a padded seat and a turn-of-the-century catalogue-ordered chair with tattered upholstery and decorative mouse-nibbled fringe. Both were rescued. We all discovered bits and pieces of discarded farm equipment which were strewn everywhere. The large pieces we painted black and used as found sculpture. Small pieces, up to 12 inches long, were also painted black and served as window stops to keep the sash windows open, or as doorstops. Other doorstops would be made by upholstering bricks with fabric remnants.

Buying second-hand furniture was another option. We bought a walnut-stained dining-room table with six matching chairs at Armstrong's Antiques—housed in a barn north of Orangeville. The price? $85.00. I varnished the table top with urethane and recovered the seats with attractive oilcloth from Finland. The chairs from this set, now padded and in their third upholstered incarnation, allow us to accommodate at least twelve at the "new" table in our "new" dining room at the Hougues Magues. Our bargain dining table is now the desk in my basement office in our Toronto home.

Then there were leftovers. The previous owners of our Toronto house had left behind a well-designed, sturdy, and very shabby three-seater couch. With a new slipcover, it served us very well for years at the farm, and now it sits in Nickie and Michael's recreation room in Toronto. The Millers' 1920s orange-painted sideboard—I think they charged us $15.00 for it—was an eyesore. Under the orange paint was oak which I oiled. It stored plates and cutlery for many years at the farm but it too has moved on to Nickie's house. Nigel painted one of the Miller's bedroom chests bright red for his bedroom and another was stripped and re-varnished; both are still in use. Then there were the dozen turquoise-painted deal chairs. My mother took this on as her personal project. Nothing is as tedious as stripping painted chairs with rungs and back spokes, but it didn't stop her. She cleaned them all. Now varnished, they have been endlessly useful.

Best of all were hand-me-downs. Pottery, mixing bowls, pie plates and blankets from the Caledon cottage; more blankets, a breadboard, a breadbox, a kitchen stool, and blue and white ceramic canisters from my mother's kitchen; and paintings from Uncle Theo. The neat thing is they were and are useful and they are forever a reminder of other places and people now gone. A lookalike of my mother's old black and white enamel breadbox recently appeared in a kitchen featured in Architectural Digest.

Brightly coloured, woven cotton rugs, purchased in Yugoslavia prior to our return home from Andrew's post-doctoral year in Paris covered the floor, or tables, or dilapidated chairs as required. Then we needed lamps. After kitchen plumbing had been installed, we painted the discarded hand pump black, wired in a socket, added a lampshade, and instantly produced a most attractive and stable lamp which is still in Nigel's bedroom at the farm. Considerably less stable, in fact very unstable, were the lamps we devised from fluted walnut table legs found in the barn, although the tabletop originally attached to them never was found. After we stripped and re-varnished the legs, Andrew drilled a hole to wire them through their centres. Once topped with lampshades, they were incongruously elegant. Unfortunately they tended to fall over every time you switched them on. So it's not surprising that Nigel and Nickie resolutely refused to provide them house room. One is gone. The other is now my desk lamp.

***

WE AVOIDED SMALL EXPENSES by not buying fast food on the way up to the farm on Friday evenings. Instead we'd eat sandwiches in the car—so often prepared by my mother when she was coming to the farm with us.

We chose to keep the party line rather than pay for a more expensive private phone line. We knew every time the phone rang that it rang in every house sharing the line, and everyone picked up their phones to listen in—but it halved the phone bill. It amused us that when we were talking on the phone, you could hear the clock chime in an eavesdropper's kitchen. Mildred Carmichael and Mary Morrison were prime offenders. It didn't bother us because we never considered anything we said to be earth-shatteringly important. Eventually the time came when we had to switch to a private line, but party lines are still in use.

We always tried to conserve electricity. In Toronto we used the clothes dryer only for towels and sheets. All the other clothes were hung out to dry on racks and hangers in the basement. Given all the lint that collects in the filter, a secondary gain from restricting the use of the dryer was that our clothes would probably last longer.

As for avoiding major expenses, we never did become a two-car family. Andrew and I both ride bicycles to work. No parking fees! The major farm expense we have avoided is the purchase of a tractor. If I were to buy a lottery ticket (which I never do), and if I were to win, the first thing I'd buy would be a proper tractor for Andrew. We've been lucky that Norm McKibbon and Don Emmerson have been so generous, lending their tractors to Andrew when he wanted to distribute fence rails or to carry loads of stones in the front-end loader. Even so, Andrew has moved most of the stones for the dry stone walls and garden rockeries using just his wheel-barrow or his lawn tractor hitched to the small wagon Nickie, then a university student, extravagantly bought for him. When we got into moving boulders (about half the size of a Volkswagen), we hired a bulldozer. A bulldozer would be fun to own—provided it never broke down.

Of course, being frugal is an easy choice when you feel secure, are healthy and have friends and family who help you. Easier than when you are living hand-to-mouth and the need to be frugal erodes your self-esteem.

HERE ARE THREE much-used recipes from the Baines' Frugal Period which are still being used by the next generation.

Guernsey Gache-May-Lah

This is a recipe from my mother and I've written it as we always pronounced it. The original words would have been Guernsey French and probably the "may-lah" originally meant *mélange*, that is to say, "a mixture."

Whatever is not eaten right away can be cut into serving size squares and frozen for subsequent use. While it is supposed to be made with apples, of which we have an endless supply at the farm, we started using pears when I became allergic to apples. Pears work just as well. As she grew older, my mother became increasingly imaginative in her cooking, and she would sometimes add chopped prune plums to the pears or apples. Sometimes she added a little cinnamon. Both Nickie and Nigel like this dessert so much they make it in large quantities for freezing, using apples from the farm.

Place leftover pastry dough in a bowl. Assess its volume. My leftover pastry usually measures about 1 cup. Chill. Peel and coarsely chop apples or pears to make a volume three times that of the pastry dough. The fruit should not be over-ripe. Depending on your taste, and the sweetness of the fruit, add about 1/2 cup sugar for the equivalent of every 3 cups of fruit. Using a sharp knife (not a pastry blender), cut the fruit into the pastry until it is finely chopped (1/4- to 3/8-inch pieces) and well mixed with the pastry. Do not let it turn into a wet ball. Spread mixture in 8x8 inch pan and bake at 400°F for 45 minutes.

When it's done, it will be golden brown on the top with delicate spicules pointing upwards. It should be served warm, not hot, with ice cream or whipped cream.

Oma's Butter Tarts

Butter tarts seem to be unique to Ontario. When I was a little girl, my mother made them regularly, her recipe coming from the brochure of a now forgotten company—Love's I think it was—that sold vanilla and spices for cooking. In my memory her butter tarts always came out of the oven just when I got home from school in the afternoon, and I was allowed to eat one while it was still slightly warm and the pastry was delicate and flaky. Ever since, I have scorned the runny, syrupy butter tarts everyone else makes. I guess it's imprinting. Or is it that I don't like syrup running down my fingers? There is *no* corn syrup in these tarts.

Prepare at least 14 large tart shells using muffin pans rather than foil tart tins. Do not be tempted to buy frozen tart shells; they are unsatisfactory. The Hougues Magues pastry recipe works well. In a bowl, beat together 1/4 cup butter with a very scant cup of white sugar. Beat in two eggs, one at a time until the batter is pale in colour. Add 1/3 tsp vanilla, and 1/2 tsp each of ground cinnamon and nutmeg. Place a scant tbsp of currants in each of the unbaked tart shells. If you wish, you can add some chopped walnuts or dried orange peel, but you will need more than 14 shells. Pour the batter into each tart shell, filling it to within 1/4 inch of the top of the pastry, no more. Bake at 375°F for 20 to 25 minutes. The tarts will puff up while cooking and then subside.

The tarts should have a firm but delicate, custard-like texture. I've never met anyone who did not like them. Indeed I remember the son of one of our guests eating about six tarts within ten minutes, leaving me quite indignant because the rest of us were deprived of seconds.

Much as I like sweets, main courses are necessary too. The Langan family was the first of all our friends to visit the farm—so early that they were there well before the closing date. Janine Langan is a fabulous cook who came from France. It was her family who had hosted

Nickie in Normandy in the summer of 1970. She too was interested in frugality because she had a large family to feed. She introduced us to a delicious main course alternative to meat.

Fried Cottage Cheese Patties

For this recipe to work, you need the dry cottage cheese that comes wrapped in paper—I've only found it at Jewish dairies. In the seventies that cheese was a lot less expensive than it is now, but then again, our salaries have increased too, so we should not complain.

Place 1lb cottage cheese in bowl. Beat 2 eggs in another bowl. Sauté one clove of chopped garlic and one medium-sized, coarsely chopped cooking onion in butter until the onion is clear but not browned. Mix into cheese. Sprinkle on top of cheese 1 heaping tbsp flour, 1 tsp salt and fresh or dried herbs such as oregano, parsley and basil to taste. Mix. Add eggs to cheese mixture and mix thoroughly. Then shape into hamburger-sized patties. If the mixture is too wet, add a little more flour. Pour fine bread crumbs on a board or a plate and coat each patty completely with crumbs. It may be helpful to chill the patties for an hour before frying. When ready to eat, sauté the patties in melted butter in a large frying pan over a very low heat, about 3 to 4 minutes each side until golden brown and heated through. Care is needed when flipping over the patties otherwise they may fall apart. You should be able to serve them intact. With relish, a salad and bread, they make a perfect meal.

Another one of our frugal meals was spaghetti meat sauce. Made in huge batches (3 pounds of lean ground beef, 3 large cans of tomatoes, 2 large cans of tomato paste, onions, celery and herbs), I made it, froze it and ate it so many times, I can't even bear to look at it now. So no recipe! But Nickie and Nigel must have liked it, because they still make it.

DESPITE ALL THIS frugality, we lived quite happily. But if we thought we were frugal, others didn't see it quite that way. Through Norm and Frieda we learned that our neighbours on the fifth line were attributing to us a quite preposterous degree of wealth. They believed that all doctors earned in excess of $100,000. Andrew and I were both doctors, therefore our combined incomes had to be more than $200,000. Nothing could have been further from the truth. I was practising medicine three mornings a week in a hospital clinic and paid meagrely on a sessional, not a fee-for-service, basis. Andrew, who had been given tenure at the University, was largely involved in research and teaching. Protestations from us would have been totally inappropriate because at the end of the day, it didn't matter what we actually earned. Compared to our neighbours, we were wealthy. If they ever noticed our frugality, it must have puzzled them. The important thing is that they always made us feel welcome.

What was also interesting were some of the comments friends from the city would make when they visited us. Upper-middle-class professionals would tell us they never could afford a farm like ours. We always managed to bite back any retorts. When a comment like this came from a surgeon (who owned a yacht with a purchase price triple that of our farm, and with annual insurance, mooring, storage and club fees well in excess of our annual farm maintenance costs; who each winter went to luxury hotels in Florida or the Caribbean; and who went away for idle summer vacations at Muskoka resorts) our suppressed exasperation is easy to understand.

The moral of the story is, of course, that very few people can have it all. Our priority was a farm for all seasons to be shared with anyone who, like us, found spiritual renewal there. Our "rest and recreation" was to embellish the house, enjoy the garden, fix fences, improve agricultural land and grow trees. And we always preferred buying theatre tickets to sending Andrew's shirts out. Still do. Different strokes for different folks. Or you could say, different priorities to meet different needs.

ANGUS MCARTHUR was frugal, too, when his house was being built, frugal both outside and in. Outside, the front façade of the house boasted cut stone blocks while the sides were made of uncut fieldstone. To give the appearance of cut stone, the mortar on the sides and back of the house was etched in horizontal and vertical lines. Inside, there was much more lavish expenditure for the main floor than for the upstairs bedrooms. The baseboards on the main floor were all a generous eleven inches high, in some rooms relatively plain and in other places, elaborate. Those on the second floor were only five inches high and all were uniformly plain. The window reveals on the main floor were made of wood while on the second floor, the reveals were just plaster. Downstairs, all the door and window frames were enhanced by moulding. No decorative moulding was used upstairs.

But even on the main floor itself, the relative importance of different rooms is clearly signalled by a hierarchy of decorative detail. In the front entrance hall and in what was the original parlour, the 11-inch baseboards are elaborate, while those in the dining room are slightly less so. In the parents' bedroom off the parlour, they are quite plain. As for the kitchen, the wainscotting renders baseboards entirely unnecessary. Similarly, the wooden window reveals are sometimes more and sometimes less extravagant. In the parlour, they are elaborately panelled as are the sidelights in the entrance hall. They are totally flat and plain in the parents' bedroom, the dining-room and the kitchen. Angus's frugality resulted in the less public parts of the house being treated a little less generously.

However, there are three features of the house which persuade me that Angus, like us, practised frugality to achieve selected extravagances. Apparently it is extremely unusual for 19th century houses in Ontario to have the date when they were built incorporated into their structure. Despite his frugality, Angus paid for an elaborate keystone. Surrounded by a raised margin, the keystone highlights the 1876 date with a scalloped pattern above the numbers and a line of small circles below. The second feature is the stone lintel above the front door.

Instead of having four corners, this lintel's two upper corners are rounded, a feature which one architect claimed never to have seen before and found very appealing. Finally, the gothic window Angus had installed is yet another extravagant gesture. At that time in Ontario, in order to pare the cost of the popular gothic-style windows, triangular window frames were commonly installed rather than curved frames. Angus went for the more expensive curved gothic window.

He never could have imagined how much we would appreciate his house with its strong sense of place, its complexity. It is full of "thereness."

Chapter 12

Nature's Bounty

*How lavish, how carelessly profuse
is nature in her handiwork.*

**Anna B. Jameson, *Winter Studies and
Summer Rambles in Canada*. 1837.**

T HE BAINES' may have been frugal, but Nature is not. She has
been lavish in her gifts to Sydenham. The land around us is
amazing. Rich pasture for livestock, fertile land for diverse
crops, plentiful firewood, timber for building, fish in rivers and lakes,
wild fowl and deer in the woods. The rugged face of the Niagara
escarpment heading north to the tip of the Bruce peninsula. The
drama of Inglis Falls as it plunges 18 metres downward into its gorge.
The frenzied determination of Chinook salmon struggling up the
Sydenham River each fall. The pleasures of Hibou Beach, sandy, sheltered and safe, a paradise for children on hot summer days. Then there
are the other treasures to be discovered on our farm.

What we live with, we don't always appreciate. Years ago, that
really struck home. One day Andrew's father, "Barge" Baines (so-
called because he tended to walk absent-mindedly into things and
people), was visiting a neighbour's farm in search of a view to paint.
The farm had been in the family for three generations and the house
looked over the Bighead Valley. "What a beautiful view!" Barge
exclaimed. "Oh!" was the surprised response from the man who had

lived there since childhood. "I'd never noticed it before." There is beauty all around us in Sydenham Township. Some see it, but don't value it. Others don't even see it.

What do we city-dwellers *see* in Sydenham? When we walk through the fields to our forest, the transition from one to the other is more than physical. The trees permit us to enter their domain. They rise tall around us, elegant, strong and welcoming. The patterns made by their spreading branches set off the beauty of the sky when we look upward. On the forest floor strange berries appear in the fall, and vines and young saplings and rotting trees are always present. It is so heavily quiet—the only sounds are those we make, or the sound of branches creaking, of leaves rustling in the wind, or the calling of birds. There is serenity in Sydenham forests. We also see the energy and the beauty of Sydenham's rivers and creeks criss-crossing the landscape and can be spellbound by the changing moods of the sweeping body of water that is Georgian Bay.

Major sources of joy are the constant vistas, encompassing sky, fields, rivers and valleys, all because Sydenham's terrain features so many hills. When we leave the farm to return to Toronto, our route always takes us up to the top of the hill where we were first introduced to the Hougues Magues. There Andrew slows the car down almost to a stop. We look southeast. Each season, each time of day reveals a different spectacle—the pale green wash of trees in early spring, the oblique rays of the setting sun in any season, sometimes heavy sullen skies, and sometimes a dramatic display of blue-black storm clouds invading the valley. Whatever we see is always inspiring.

In the winter, Sydenham is a world of white, interrupted by leafless trees just like a David Milne landscape. Evergreens, bright sun and blue skies make the starkness bearable. Soft pillows of snow rest on large rocks in our fence-rows and more snow settles comfortably on the branches of tall trees in the woods, plopping down on cross-country skiers if the wind rises even slightly. Behind bushes, grouse rise suddenly and startle skiers with their loud flutterings. Under bridges of ice and snow, our creek rushes noisily to the big pond, or further, to the Bighead River. Sometimes we see a coyote gravely staring at us no more than 30 feet away. Footprints from deer and rabbits are everywhere. In our forest the deer strip the lower branches of our tamarack trees leaving needles and twigs in the trampled snow underneath. Around the house they eat the yews, the euonymus and the rhododendrons and even nibble the ivy on the walls. Very often early in the morning, when we are drinking cappuccino in bed (I'm spoiled by my husband), we will see as many as a dozen deer bounding effortlessly over our snow-covered fields.

Then come the muddy times of early spring—mud on the roads, mud on the car, mud on the paths, mud on our boots. My mother's opinion was that "there are no wildflowers in Canada." She remembered Guernsey woods carpeted with bluebells and primroses in the spring. Instead, here in Sydenham woods, we enjoy white and mauve wood violets, Johnny Jump-ups and trilliums. Marsh marigolds flourish wherever there is marshy land. Spring's dandelions I will not praise. In May on "Arbour Day"—a day for promoting appreciation for trees that has been part of the school calendar for more than a hundred years in Ontario—Betty Murdoch used to take her class to our woods where they would find wild orchids. We have found Lady's Slipper, one of forty orchid species indigenous to the area. Ferns are profligate. Wild ginger can be found in the woods and so can wild leeks. Don Emmerson picks wild leeks every spring, and Lois boils them for supper. Later, gigantic puffballs are easily found (delicious when sliced and fried in butter). When the elm trees were still around, Andrew found morels in their shadow—but no longer. Spring is also when the fishing season starts, and cars line the roads around the Bighead River so fishermen can catch brown and speckled trout.

The goldfinches return wearing winter's drab wardrobe. Gradually, as we watch them visiting our feeders, they change to summer yellow. They are joined by purple finches who aren't remotely purple, Baltimore orioles, scarlet tanagers, killdeer, barn swallows, rose-breasted grosbeaks, and mourning doves. Cardinals and blue jays are always around. Sometimes the cardinals disturb us because they repeatedly hurl themselves at our windows. The blue jays have an ugly squawk and are pushy at the feeders. Year after year, a pair of phoebes builds their nest just above the verandah door. We put up with their white droppings on the step below until the nest is empty of chicks. Robins hop about on the lawn looking for worms, oblivious of the fact that my mother scorned them for being too large and awkward. Sparrows are busybodies and chickadees are cute. Later the hummingbirds will come, and up on Norm and Frieda's old farm, bluebirds nest. With our binoculars we can watch disdainful hawks and the sinister silhouettes of turkey vultures soaring high above our little valley.

When summer arrives, we stay out of the woods. The insects keep us out, so we find our pleasures elsewhere. Andrew keeps hunting mushrooms and in July may find chanterelles. Apple trees have grown up all over the farm, species whose names we do not know. There are apples with flesh as white as snow, sweet and crisp, which have to be eaten the day they are picked. Others are keepers. The variety of textures and tastes is astonishing. It's a nuisance not being able to eat apples when they're so plentiful. Many ways to cook them can be found in the Ginger Press publication *Reds of Grey: A Collection of Apple Recipes from Grey County Kitchens* (1995). Watercress can be picked in the creek and wild mint grows in patches on the banks. There are wild grapes to pick, but they don't tempt us. The roadsides and the fields are full of wildflowers: purple crown vetch, orange lilies, blue cornflowers, delicate white Queen Anne's lace, and goldenrod.

When evening has wrapped all the flowers in darkness, we stand outside and watch fireflies by the thousands as they flicker and flash with silent energy over low-lying fields.

Nigel collects apples for cooking.

IN 1980 Norm and Frieda decided to sell their farm and move into Owen Sound. Around the same time, Janos and Lou decided to sell their place as well. Janos put an advertisement in a German newspaper where it was found by a Swiss couple, Walter and Sigi Blaesi. Eventually Walter and Sigi would prove to appreciate Nature's summer bounty as much as Andrew and I do, but at the time I only saw them as agents of unwanted change. After talking to Janos in Vienna, Walter decided to fly to Canada to look at the farm. As a friend of the Hrabovszkys, I was enlisted to assist them in the enterprise by driving this "interloper" (as I then thought of him) to the farm. Walter inspected the old house without a morsel of enthusiasm. Although it was beautifully situated overlooking the Queen's Valley, it truly was in a neglected state. Janos and Lou had never stayed there for more than a few days at a time and then only infrequently. We had ignored the handwriting on the wall because we hoped after Janos retired they would be coming for prolonged periods of time. It wasn't to be. Janos wanted to sell but clearly Walter was not going to buy.

Before the long drive back to Toronto, hospitality required that I drive Walter over to the Hougues Magues for a cup of coffee. As I drove up the fifth line, Walter noticed the McKibbons' "For Sale" sign at the top of the hill and asked to go in. With extreme reluctance (I really didn't want Norm and Frieda to sell and hoped they would change their minds), I turned the car into their long lane and drove up to the house. Walter probably decided to buy their farm almost as quickly as I had decided to buy ours, in both instances, absent our spouses. Janos would not be thrilled with this turn of events. I wasn't either. I wanted the McKibbons to stay, but they didn't. They moved to Owen Sound. The Blaesis moved in and Janos and Lou found another buyer for their farm.

How wrong I had been! After Sigi's initial discombobulation (the first night she spent at "Walter's Farm" was so black and the farm so isolated, she was amazed anyone could have lived there), she and Walter settled right in. They have been a joy to have as neighbours, not just for us, but for people far and wide in the township and beyond. They display extraordinary energy, enthusiasm, generosity and hospitality. Then there is Walter's music. A self-taught musician, he plays alpenhorn, trumpet and piano. If he brings his accordion to a party it has a magical effect—the liveliness index goes way up. Since they took early retirement from their business in Switzerland, Walter and Sigi spend May to October in Sydenham and the remainder of the year in Europe at their homes in Switzerland and Austria.

It's interesting for a Canadian to hear Europeans reacting to the land around us, in particular, to Sydenham. Countless times Walter has expostulated (because that is how he talks) about how won-der-ful-l-l it is to own land in Sydenham, a place he chose only after rejecting properties on the eastern seaboard and in the American

Midwest. What appeals to him is the space, the clean air, the silence, the privacy, the freedom from excessive regulation, and the beauty of the landscape. Of course, we agree with him completely. Walter is very astute.

Every morning just at sunrise, Sigi walks to a rise on their land, marked by a tree around which Walter built a bench. There she watches the sun climb into Sydenham skies above the Bighead Valley. The valley can be drowned in mist, appearing from her perch like a vast lake with the distant hills enclosing it. Each evening, after dinner, she and Walter walk to the same rise of land and watch the day ending, so often in a blaze of colour. When dark falls, they watch the skies and count the shooting stars. For them the land and being outdoors are of paramount importance. Both are exceptional athletes and in Sydenham they can play tennis and golf, swim in their pond and bicycle over the country roads. A short drive takes them for a day of sun at beautiful Sauble Beach in neighbouring Bruce County. Their comfortable house is the venue for their exceptional hospitality, extended not only to Sydenham residents but also to literally dozens of European visitors, friends and family, who come every year to enjoy "Walter's Farm."

Sigi, an Austrian, brings with her many customs which were probably familiar in rural Ontario several generations ago, but now are largely forgotten. Her folklore tells her one phase of the moon is right for weeding, another is right for planting, and still another right for pruning trees and mowing the grass. My great grandfather Guillaume Nicolle (who owned a warehouse and supervised shipments of Guernsey fruit and vegetables daily to Covent Garden in London) probably would have known all this too. My mother told me he always went out to bow three times to a new moon. (In Alistair MacLeod's novel *No Great Mischief*, he describes a character who would "bow or almost curtsey to the new moon" while saying

"Glory forever to thee so bright
Thou moon so white of this very night;

Thouself forever thou dost endure
as the glorious lantern of the poor.")

While Sigi doesn't bow to the moon, she does respect the impact of phases of the moon. She also knows how to benefit from what to so many of us are just generic weeds. She harvests them in the fields and makes delicious herbal teas and soothing oils for scratches and bites. Unquestionably, Sigi recognizes Nature's Bounty.

Sigi's Herbal Tea

Pick St. John's Wort in June when the flowers are blooming—not too early in the morning because the flowers must be dry, but certainly no later than 3:00 o'clock in the afternoon. Hang in bunches by the stems in a cool dry place, out of the sun. When thoroughly dried, remove the blossoms. They come off easily. Mix the blossoms with dried lavender, sage, mint and thyme, all three of which should be dried the same way as the St. John's Wort. Pour boiling water on the dried herbs and steep 5 minutes to make your tea.

Sigi's Soothing Oil

This is very comforting when applied to scratches, rashes and insect bites.

Pick St. John's Wort as described above. Remove the fresh blossoms and pack tightly into a small jar. Half fill the jar with a good quality olive oil. Place the jar outside where it will get maximum sun exposure and leave it for two weeks. After two weeks, the oil will be a deep red. Strain and store in tightly sealed jars.

***

FALL COMES and the fields and ditches are full of blooms and grasses suitable for making winter bouquets. We bring in grapevines to wind into wreaths. Pine-cones are collected for Christmas. The leaves turn colour and the hunting season starts. Our friend Joe Da Silva comes up from Toronto with his youngest son Andrew to stay in our house and hunt deer. I'm always glad we are not around for the mid-week hunting which goes on all around the farm. However, this area is overpopulated with deer so I wish the hunters luck.

Then we are back to winter. We never need a refrigerator to chill our champagne on New Year's Eve.

Chapter 13

One Step at a Time

Our drawing room was just completed before Christmas Day
and I assure you no little admiration has been bestowed upon it.
I do not mean by guests, though no doubt they did admire;
but it was from our self-satisfied selves that the exclamation
"What a pretty room!" has burst forth.

Letter from Anne Langton, January 1, 1839.

I F, WHEN WE BOUGHT the farm, we had been shown a list of all the things we would eventually do to the house and land, we would have snorted with disbelief. Spend all that money? We didn't have it! Work so hard? We weren't going to become slaves to property management! But nobody told us what the future held and we never thought further ahead than one step at a time. We always believed that after a specific project was completed, there really wouldn't be much more to do. How naïve we were.

There were leaks everywhere, so a first priority had to be to close off unused chimneys, put on a new roof, and replace windows with rotted frames, of which, thank goodness, there were very few. That done, we could turn to more appealing projects.

KITCHENS ARE IMPORTANT rooms, especially large kitchens that have a fireplace and serve as your dining-room. So in the beginning we focused a lot on what we wanted to do with the kitchen. After the installation of the kitchen plumbing, we needed to build a counter. Spending more money to buy a prefabricated counter never entered our minds. Outside, Andrew had dismantled an old chicken shed which had been made with 4x8 sheets of plywood. The plywood was filthy, covered with dried chickenshit. After a thorough hosing and scrubbing with bleach, the wood was ready for recycling as the counter top. That it was slightly warped didn't bother us. Scavenging more lumber from the barn, we built a frame for the counter. The next thing we needed was something reasonably attractive to close off one long side and two short ends, something for a countertop which would be both waterproof and cleanable, and finally, some cabinet doors for the fourth side. We ended up buying only the hardware for the doors and floor tiles for the countertop.

To cover the long side facing the fireplace as well as the two ends, we used barn-boards which Andrew's brother-in-law Neville Lyon found for us. (Neville, a Brit and therefore particular about such things, always corrected me if I referred to him as my brother-in-law. He was not *my* brother-in-law, he would explain patiently, because he was married to Andrew's sister. Because I am an only child, it was disappointing to be limited to just one sister-in-law.) As for the barn-boards, all we had to do was pick them up in Belfountain, which was almost on the way to the farm from Toronto anyway. To match the gray, weathered barn-boards, we chose pale gray vinyl floor tiles for the countertop, which cost around 15 cents a square foot. Self-adhesive, they were easily installed and stuck firmly to the cleaned plywood from the chicken shed. Aluminum trim around the counter margins probably cost us at most a few dollars. The barn-boards have long since gone and so have the vinyl tiles. But the cabinet doors we contrived remain with us to this day.

When we bought our 20-foot-wide, three-story, semi-detached Toronto house, it was riddled with small dark rooms shut off from each other by darkly varnished doors in darkly varnished frames, with halls covered in deep-toned, silver-flecked, floral wallpaper. You could not enter it without thinking "Light, light, light, please!" So one of the first things we did was remove doors and take down walls. But being frugal, we did not throw out the doors. When we needed kitchen cabinet doors at the farm, we examined the doors from the house and realized what wonderful things could be done with them. The dark varnish was easily removed and beneath we found lovely honey-coloured pine. It matched the pine wainscotting we were uncovering in the Hougues Magues.

The salvaged doors had been made long before slab doors were introduced to the market. As is quite usual for older doors, there was a single short horizontal panel at the top of the door, and two long parallel vertical panels below the upper panel. This arrangement met our needs perfectly. We sawed off the top third of the door, the section with the horizontal panel. This section, if stood vertically, became a very attractive kitchen cabinet door.

Four such doors were made, varnished, hinged, adorned with neat white porcelain knobs and hung from the counter. They've been there ever since. Even though I still believe this was a brilliant innovation, to my knowledge, no one has ever followed our example. Which only goes to show how brilliant ideas are often appreciated only by their creators.

Before long, we would replace Neville's barn board when serendipity once again intervened. One day, driving into town, I noticed that the nearby stone schoolhouse just to the north of us, "SS No. 11, Sydenham Fifth Line," was being gutted by its owner to modernize the interior. Piled by the road, waiting to be disposed of, were brown-painted boards, wainscotting from the classroom. These would have been installed in 1875, the year before our house was built. Although I did not know the owner, I knocked on the door and asked

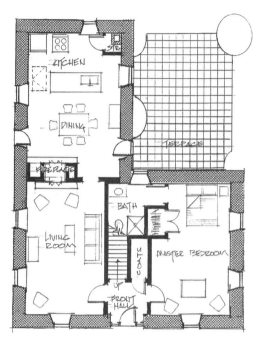

1st Floor

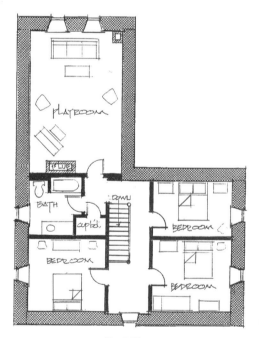

2nd Floor

1975 House layout.
Drawn by George Yost.

for the boards. He was delighted to have them taken off his hands. So Andrew and I collected all the boards and took them back to the Hougues Magues. After the old nails were removed and the paint stripped, they were exactly what we needed. Now the wood on our counter was a perfect match for our kitchen wainscotting and our recycled cabinet doors.

As for the vinyl, it had served us very well but it looked out of place with the pine boards. We chose some ceramic tiles to replace the vinyl—of course in mid-winter—so that Andrew had the pleasure of hauling the heavy boxes (at least they were small) to the house on skis. It wasn't much work to lay them, even though the plywood from the chicken shed had not lost its warp. To finish the edges, Andrew installed butternut moulding which he had planed himself.

But long before the schoolhouse boards found a new home on our counter, we tackled another major job in the kitchen. That was the removal of the east wall—the wall with the two doors, the wall with the rat's nest and the silver spoon. Behind that wall, we had to remove the staircase that went up to the second floor playroom. What a mess plaster and lath and studs make when you tear them down! However, the reward was more floor space and an extra window in the kitchen.

Given the power outages that occur in the winter, we needed a fireplace. While we were delighted to get rid of wood-stoves and gain the space they had occupied, we needed a backup for when our furnace couldn't run. But there could be no fireplace until Andrew moved a doorway. The door leading from the kitchen to the living-room was centrally placed in the wall and had to be shifted to the left to make room for the fireplace. Andrew carefully took apart and re-installed the old pine door-frames on each side of the wall. Then we installed an unnecessarily large prefabricated fireplace, a Heatilator. Equipped with glass doors on both sides—to the kitchen and to the living-room—ducts from the Heatilator also warmed the upstairs. It had a huge capacity for large logs that quickly coated our chimney with pitch, leading to one very noisy chimney fire. Although we hired someone to build the chimney and the brick surround for the fire-place, it was Andrew who designed and made the mantels for the two sides of the fireplace, in both instances using old pine. On the living-room side, the mantel-piece was embellished with three old walnut carvings from my father, a bird and two rosettes—medallions he must have removed from some old furniture.

Meantime Nickie and I were spending hours stripping paint off all the wainscotting in the kitchen. That proved to be the easiest of all our paint removal jobs because the Millers had already burned off the thick old layers of paint with a blowtorch and then painted it turquoise. Even though there was only one layer of paint, it still wasn't easy because the beading in the wainscotting retained some of the old paint and there were burn marks to sand away. I think it was Mel Morrison who arrived at this point and asked us what colour we were going to paint the wood. Apparently the 19th century disdain for pine as a "cheap" wood to be hidden had been transmitted to a third gener-ation. This disdain for pine explains why on all the rest of the pine in the house, we found a thin layer of hard white plaster on which an ugly faux oak grain had been painted. Later residents apparently didn't like the faux grain either, accounting for the many layers of paint.

Eventually the pine in the kitchen was clean and smooth enough to varnish. Andrew's mother paid for new kitchen linoleum patterned like Italian ceramic tile, a big improvement on the plywood flooring. (It was plywood because Norm had lifted the original kitchen flooring and put it in the living room. Because he had used the kitchen as a woodshed, it didn't need the good floor.) Then we chose a nice new wallpaper for the kitchen—which I hung—and it's been there ever since. Presto! Our first beautiful room.

❦

OVER A PERIOD of about 12 years, we all worked endless hours stripping the interior wood of paint. The best way proved to be a hand-held heating element that melted the paint. Nickie and I, inured to the characteristic acrid burning smell, used putty knives to scrape the softened paint off the flat areas and steel dinner knives to pry paint out of the grooves and curves in the moulding. The trick of course was to avoid burning the wood (or yourself) with the element and to prevent the knives from gouging the wood. At this point Andrew would take over and with more enduring muscle power, sand the rough surface of the wood until it was smooth and completely clean. My job was to do the fine sanding and varnishing. We restored the natural pine not only in the kitchen, but also in the front entrance, and in the then first-floor master bedroom.

Downstairs, the warm honey tones of the original eleven-inch pine baseboards, the doors and the two beautifully panelled window reveals remain a constant pleasure—worth all the work. When we wanted to extend the cleaning process to the stairs and the upstairs doors, doorframes and windowsills, we decided we'd had enough, and hired someone else to complete the job.

But before we sought that outside help, we had already sanded and varnished the floors, upstairs and down. Most of the floors had been painted an unattractive and rather shiny yellowy-brown with buttermilk paint. This paint proved impervious to our heating element as well as to any chemical we ever applied. The only way we could get rid of it was with a power sander. Is it the protein in the milk that makes it so indestructible? We were told that the paint was made by stirring some mustard into a bucket of buttermilk and waiting for it to set. Whatever the formula, it was unassailable. So we rented a huge floor sander, opened the windows, wore masks, covered our hair and started pushing. That I was an amateur as a floor sander is evident by the gouges I put in the broad pine plank flooring and the small triangles of buttermilk paint which remain intact to this day in some corners. But despite all these flaws, the sanded and varnished floors were a great improvement. Floor sanding is the most dusty and noisy of a renovator's jobs. Floor varnishing, on the other hand, is the most frustrating because it's so difficult to get rid of all the particles that hover in the air waiting to settle on a freshly varnished surface before it dries.

***

"THAT IS NOT ALL, oh no, that is not all." I keep thinking of Dr. Seuss as I write because in this first phase of our renovations there remains much to be chronicled: work on the front hall, reconstruction of the parlour, revision of the lying-in room, re-configuration of the upstairs bedrooms and the rehabilitation of the playroom.

Our first living-room, the room adjacent to the kitchen, required the least effort of all the rooms in the house. It had to be painted after we removed the wallpaper. Scars on the ceiling where Norm had removed the rosette needed smoothing over. Once the wood-stove was replaced by the fireplace, the hole in the ceiling from the stove-pipe had to be closed. Then there was a doorway to wall in. Immediately to the left on entry from the kitchen, was a door into a small room whose original purpose may well have been a lying-in room for mothers immediately after childbirth. Frieda made it her kitchen because the kitchen proper was their woodshed. Because we intended to use the original parlour and the room beyond it on the other side of the house as our master bedroom, we shut the original entrance to Frieda's kitchen and opened up a door on the opposite side so the room could serve as our *en suite* bathroom. Compared to what we did in other rooms, this was accomplished in the flick of an eyelash. Of course it helped that we decided not to strip the wood-work in the living-room. The window reveals and the baseboards are still painted off-white.

From the living-room to the front hall. For a long time, rain had been entering through the un-puttied panes of the transom, staining the hardwood floor with unsightly water marks. One of my first projects was to extract from the transom frame the panes of old glass with their lovely irregular swirls; to chip out whatever old, hard putty remained on the frame and the glass; and to re-install the panes and sand and varnish the wood frame. At a much later stage we would get rid of the thick white paint riddled with cracks that covered the rest of the wood in the hall.

Then there was the issue of cupboard space. Why were so many rural Ontario houses built without cupboards? There wasn't one cupboard in the house. Perhaps they used wardrobes. In-season clothes were probably hung on wall hooks. Most of the rooms, all but the parlour and dining-room, had a three-inch pine board set into the wall about 6 feet above the floor with clothes hooks screwed into them. We wanted cupboards, not wall hooks, and not wardrobes. Norm's whim so long ago which had led him to enclose the parlour alcove, provided an opportunity for us to create a hall closet. Andrew accessed that closed space from the front hall by opening up a new doorway. He installed a pine doorframe and recycled a pine door. We now had a hall cupboard for boots and coats—and as a bonus we retrieved the long-trapped yellow-painted chair which my mother proceeded to strip.

The original parlour was a small room, one of two on the south side of the house. Its special status was revealed by fancier baseboards on the floor and more elaborate reveals for its two windows, compared with the room beyond which I suspect served as the parents' bedroom for both the McArthurs and the Morrisons. Norm had replaced the doorway between the two rooms with an arched space. Now we would go one step further and remove what was left of the wall to make a much larger room. At the end of this room was the newly-made doorway exiting from the original lying-in room. This tiny room had sufficient space to allow the installation of a three-piece bathroom as well as a clothes closet opening directly into our new bedroom. That bedroom taught me how to hang nine-foot lengths of wallpaper, which would not be replaced until the fall of 1998.

UPSTAIRS THERE WERE four small bedrooms over the main part of the house and the rather dismal, dark, fire-damaged and low-ceilinged room over the kitchen, destined to be the playroom (we always called it the barn-board room). In the past, this room would properly have been called the "bunkie," and originally could only have been accessed by stairs from the kitchen. By the time we purchased the house, a doorway had been made through the thick stone wall, allowing entry from the bunkie into the second floor of the main house.

We decided major changes were needed. The first was to improve access to the playroom. After we had taken out the back stairs in the kitchen, the only way to reach it was by circumnavigation— through the upstairs hall, the northwest bedroom and then the adjacent northeast bedroom. New doorways had to be opened and old ones closed off. Andrew opened up a new doorway in the hall, right at the top of the stairs, permitting direct entry into the northeast bedroom. Then he walled off the door between the two bedrooms. That done, we proceeded with the second change. Andrew partitioned the northeast bedroom (now with access to both the hall and the playroom), into a third closet, a bathroom and a small hallway.

When the second-floor bathroom was put in, we remained true to our frugal principles! Our cabinet doors were recycled from the tiny pantry in our Toronto house.

Nigel, at age 16 became the independent contractor for the cupboard in the hall outside the second-floor bathroom. In June 1979, I wrote in my diary: *Nigel has worked steadily at his upstairs storage cupboard, first fitting the plaster-board and filling the cracks, then building the door-frame, cleaning the door, hanging the door, and painting the walls inside.* The door-frame is unique. It lacks mitred corners, but it boasts a dovetailed joint right in the middle of the upper part of the frame. That's a permanent fixture. The only help he got was from his grandfather, stripping the door. My diary notes: *This weekend Opa has spent all his time working with Nigel on cleaning the door. Opa volunteered he was "having fun." That this is so remarkable to us, is sad.*

My father taught me how to use a hammer and saw, and how important it was to sandpaper wood and coats of paint thoroughly. He made several fine pieces of furniture, but eventually his compulsion to do everything properly prevented him from embarking on new projects, so intimidating was the burden of his standards. With much lower standards, Andrew and I made and refinished many pieces of furniture. Now Nigel makes beautiful furniture for his own home. Both Nickie and Nigel have undertaken the renovation of old homes with their spouses. It obviously runs in the family.

Change number three, accomplished mainly by Nigel and Nickie, was to make the playroom habitable. They began by knocking down all the cracked and charred plaster. We hired someone to put up a new ceiling and then Andrew and the children panelled the walls with barn-board. After that Nickie and I laid 4x8 plywood flooring over the damaged floors, so badly repaired after the long-ago fire. Indoor-outdoor carpeting on top of the plywood finished the room off. For many years the room was great for games, provided sleeping space for extra guests and served as a nursery for new babies.

Only one thing was left to do upstairs and that was wallpapering. Pretty, but very inexpensive wallpaper was chosen for the second-floor bedrooms and the new bathroom. The hall was painted antique white, but only after Andrew repaired countless cracks in walls and ceiling with tape and taping compound. Another unfavourite job.

THEN THERE WAS the UFFI episode—urea-formaldehyde foam insulation. UFFI seemed to us to be just what we needed to conserve energy and make the house warmer. Up until then we had used fibre-glass batts and mica. Batts were miserable to install; they got damp, and mice tore them to shreds to line their own nests. The irresistible incentive to install UFFI was that government grants, this time federal, were being offered. A local company owned by Dick Murdoch's son-in-law installed it. The bad news was that UFFI had to be blown into the spaces between the plaster and the stones where it solidified, so our walls, windowsills and the wallpaper were all punctured, leaving holes one inch in diameter that had to be plastered over. The good news was that the house was noticeably less drafty and much warmer.

Before very long a public outcry erupted claiming that people in UFFI homes were being poisoned by its vapours. No such complaints were made in Europe where UFFI is widely used, nor did people in Canada stop driving cars or throw out synthetic carpets and upholstered furniture—all of which emit similar gases. In response, the government offered more grants—this time either to remove all the UFFI in the home or to seal it in. We were in no mood to gut the house, especially since we had noted no ill effects, so we proceeded with the second choice—sealing. It was done. Under the circumstances, we really had no choice.

So disadvantageous now is UFFI to the value of a house, that a minor reduction in the residential tax rate is applied to homes with UFFI. When such a house comes up for sale, it is mandatory for the vendor to inform any potential buyer of the "problem." To this day, any house which contains UFFI, sealed or not, has a discounted value at time of sale.

***

BY 1973 the original barn was disintegrating before our eyes. It was unrescuable. Located in a damp spot, the foundations were severely cracked, the walls were beginning to list, and barn-boards were falling off. It would soon be unsafe. Before this happened, we hired Norm to dismantle it, build a new foundation on drier ground, and erect a one-and-a-half story barn using the original barn frame.

Since then we've learned a lot about barns and wonder whether we would have been wiser to choose another course. What we know now is that when we purchased the farm we became the owners of an

"English" barn measuring 35' x 56' on a raised stone foundation and with a central ramp. Because it had a gabled roof (a simple triangle), it was built before 1880. After that date, Ontario barns tended to have hipped gambrel roofs. It is very likely that our barn had been built before 1876 because barns were usually built before the house.

Originally, a barn was a place to store grain and fodder as reflected by the name's Anglo-Saxon origins—"bere" meaning barley and "ern" meaning place. As long as the English barn rested on the ground (and not on a foundation), its function remained close to its original meaning. Typically the barn would have three bays along the side, each about 15 feet wide. The central bay was used for threshing and winnowing grain and the side bays were used for storage. Up above, under the rafters, was the hayloft.

However farmers in Ontario soon learned that unlike in England, winter shelter was essential for their livestock. Unsheltered animals ate twice as much food as sheltered ones and lost weight into the bargain. In 19th century Ontario, winter feeding of livestock was said to be so inadequate that "unless the sun was shining very bright, it took two cows to make one shadow." At the same time, the farmers' families were often going hungry too, sometimes having nothing but porridge to eat, three times a day.

The need for shelter led to an adaptation of the English barn. And so our barn, like many others, may have been raised on a stone foundation some time after it was first built. In effect, the stone foundation provided a basement to the barn which functioned as a "byre," a place where livestock has traditionally been housed. Over the years cows, horses, pigs and chickens must have lived there. But a raised barn required the building of a ramp up to the central bay so wagons could bring grain in for threshing. Because our barn did not have wagon doors on both sides of the central bay, the wagons when unloaded would have had to back down the ramp to get out of the barn.

The three bays were created by four "bents," each bent being made of two posts and a tie-beam joined at right angles. The timbers

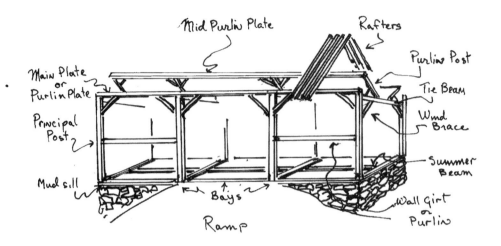

Barn Structure.
Drawn by Andrew Baines.

were held together by a mortice (a pocket in the wood) and a tenon (a projection which fitted into the mortice), the join stabilized by a "treenail" (pronounced "trunnel"). The wood of choice for trunnels was black locust which was indigenous to the area—unlike honey locusts, the trees sold to farmers as living fences. Single bents were placed at the ends of the barn, while two bents divided the long axis of the barn into thirds. All the bents and beams and purlins (beams running the length of the roof, resting on the rafters) in our barn were hand-hewn, the adze marks still visible. Posts were made of beech (our forest still has many beech) while purlins were made of hemlock and white pine—species prevalent 140 years ago. Rafters were made of saplings stripped of their bark.

Interestingly, Angus McArthur seems to have cut more corners building the barn than he did building the house. He did not bother to have all his beams and purlins stripped of bark, nor were they all squared. And there were no decorative features at all.

I don't know how many barns Norm McKibbon raised in his life, but enough that he knew how to dismantle ours very quickly. Almost too quickly. It was very unsettling when we arrived one week-

Barn roof frame with Andrew inspecting progress.

end to find that the barn had vanished completely. The foundations had been buried along with a number of artifacts we would rather have kept like the stencilled winnower and our yellow enamelled summer stove. They are buried with the stone foundations. But the dismantled timber-frame and siding were neatly laid out in the field and a concrete foundation had been poured at the new site.

Everyone except Andrew, who couldn't get away from Toronto, came up in midweek to watch the new barn being raised. Each timber of the frame had its own name and Norm was supervising men who knew these names as well as he did. Once the frame was raised, it took little time to replace the vertical siding and install a metal roof. Ironically, even on its new site, the barn foundation has cracked.

Winter is hard on people and buildings.

Chapter 14

Farming 101

The land has a miserable appearance when first cleared,
the surface and stumps being as black as fire can render them,
and these latter standing three feet high to facilitate their being drawn out
by two yoke of oxen when their roots decay,
which does not take effect for seven or eight years...

Letter IV from Thomas W. Magrath, January, 1832.
In *Authentic Letters from Upper Canada.*

IGHT FROM THE beginning, Andrew and I both believed that owning a farm obliged us to be responsible custodians, to farm one way or another. The big question was what would we do? Andrew had spent childhood summers helping on a farm near Caledon Lake, so he (unlike me) understood what haying and threshing were all about, had driven a tractor and knew how to build fences. But our land was going to be a challenge. Janos took one look at the hills, rocks and boulders in early 1971 and, with his expertise in agriculture, said, "Forget it. With this land, you'll never make any money farming." Well, we never actually expected to make money farming. We just wanted to restore the land to some kind of usefulness without losing any money in the process.

In the beginning there were no difficult decisions to make. Norm McKibbon wanted to continue renting our land to graze his beef cattle and that was great for us. Around Bognor, beef cattle were called "cattlebeasts." I rapidly learned not to call them cows, because cows are milked and cattlebeasts aren't. Cattlebeasts are gelded bulls, otherwise known as steers. Farmers around here, unless they were breeding their own herds, bought "spring feeders" at the Keady auction. These were Western cattle that had been rounded up, probably in Alberta, never having bonded in any way with human beings. They were shipped by rail to Ontario and by the time they arrived at Keady, they were socially dysfunctional and often had shipping fever. After several summers of living with Norm's cattle on the land, we decided that we'd buy a dozen cattlebeasts—Herefords—of our own.

I don't really know how we were ever brave enough (or stupid enough) to make this high risk/low benefit investment. A single strike of lightning had killed three of Norm's cattle by the avenue of cherry trees behind the house and he had had to bury them. Countless times his cattle escaped—often because people coming to the farm would breach country etiquette and leave the gates open. Several times thieves were reported to have come in the night and butchered a single beast by the roadside, leaving only hooves, entrails and head behind—although that never happened to cattle on our land. Then there was foot rot. The cattle would have to be "needled"—Norm did it himself or sometimes the local vet would have to come at no small expense. Another farmer warned us about "cattle dying of hardware." This happens when cattle eat metal objects hidden in the hay. The remedy we were told was prophylactic magnets. The cow swallows the magnet, which supposedly remains in the stomach catching the hardware and preventing it from wandering elsewhere.

Undismayed by all these problems, we went with Norm to the Keady Auction and there we stood with all the other farmers (I being the only woman there), eyeing the lots of cattle as they were brought bawling noisily into the ring. We didn't know a good beast from a bad one, but Norm did, and he chose about twelve for us. Then a truck had to be hired to take our very first cattle to the farm. When the driver arrived at our place with the cattle, he released them into the fields.

Our ridiculously solemn cattlebeasts.

What a disaster! These cattlebeasts had been confined in small spaces for at least two weeks. Once out in the fields they exulted in their freedom. They certainly were not going to let any human get near them. The cattle should have been unloaded in the barnyard so that we could have made preliminary acquaintance with them! More importantly, in the first few days we could have seen if any of them had shipping fever and treated it.

We were lucky that first year and for several years thereafter as we seemed to do all the right things and encountered no disasters. We hung a back rubber from a tree. The cattle could walk under it and the insecticide released from it would relieve their torment from the flies always swarming around them. Norm told us to buy minerals and an iodized salt-lick and put them in the barnyard. This strategy should have saved us from having to round them up in the fields, but it didn't always.

Any notion of cooing "cobossy" and developing meaningful relationships with docile cattlebeasts soon vanished. These cattle were unruly and as skittish as a flock of wild birds. We'd just look at them and they'd stampede off to the other side of the field. If we were lucky, they would not charge through the fences. If we avoided looking at them, they became pathologically curious and would noiselessly sidle up to the fence surrounding the house and watch what was going on. They were irresistibly attracted to my father's Peugeot, always so clean and carefully polished, and always parked just outside the fence. Soberly and thoroughly the cattlebeasts, having surrounded the car, would lick it, time after time, putting my father in a state of puzzled exasperation.

Still, there is something very satisfying about seeing your own cattle on your own fields. Each spring we would spend close to $10,000 on cattle and each fall we would make a profit of several hundred dollars. But owning cattle who babysit themselves Monday to Friday, leads to perpetual and well-justified anxiety, even though we knew Norm would keep an eye on them for us. Every Friday evening as we approached the farm, our hearts were always in our mouths. Would they all be there? Would they be healthy?

⟡

WELL, IN 1979, everything went wrong. My diary for May, 1979 records: *Andrew diagnosed one case of shipping fever early this morning, called the vet and then to his chagrin, was unable to produce the beast when the vet arrived extremely promptly. After trying to capture the beast for two hours (the animal took refuge in the pond), Nigel persuaded it to leave by throwing logs in the water. Andrew finally called Lloyd Carmichael for help. Lloyd brought a strong rope to lasso the animal, which then was dragged to the barn by the tractor. Once in the barn, the animal collapsed and looked terminally ill.*

Eventually the vet reappeared, gave the patient intravenous antibiotics followed by some delayed-release oral medication. He inspected the remaining cattle and said two more had shipping fever. One of these has been cajoled into the barn by Nigel who has displayed a remarkable ability to be friendly with these cattle—he even pats their hind quarters.

However the second animal remains unseducible and so he is still free in the fields. Andrew will have to stay at the farm to give more medication on Monday.

Worse was to come. Early in June, my diary continues: *Frieda phoned us in the city. A man from the Ontario Ministry of Natural Resources who had been inspecting our trees, had noticed one of our cattle-beasts was sick and lying in the pond. Thence began long-distance management devolving all responsibility onto our neighbours. The vet was called to see the beast which Don Emmerson had brought in from the pond and to which Frieda brought hay and water. By the time we arrived on the weekend, Andrew found a sick cattlebeast in the barn, another one sick and still roaming (which of course refused to be captured), and a third dead in the fields.*

In August that year, Bognor was hit by a minor hurricane. When Andrew arrived the weekend of the 20th, he found two of our cattle had gone missing, a gate was open, rail fences were scattered across the fields, our pear tree was uprooted, branches of other trees littered the lawn, and everything growing in the garden was smashed down—but the good news was some dead elms had come crashing down, saving us the trouble of felling them. Don's crop of barley was "threshed down to the ground." Two of our cattle were found on Mel Morrison's farm and he was very upset—he didn't like uninvited cattlebeasts any more than we did.

By fall we had lost two cattlebeasts. Two challenges remained. The first was to decide which week to ship the cattle back to Keady's to be sold. The prices on offer fluctuated wildly, and as usual, we relied on Norm to advise us. After he had named the date to sell, that's when we faced our second challenge: making sure the cattle would be in the barnyard when the truck arrived. The Keady Auction operated on Tuesdays. So after work on the Monday evening, Andrew and I drove up to the farm. The truck was scheduled to come early in the morning. By 6 a.m., when the cattle weren't licking the salt blocks in the barnyard as Norm had predicted, Andrew and I set out for the backfields, determined to bring the cattlebeasts back to the barn. They were equally determined to stay in the fields. The early morning light over the Valley, the cold wet grass in the fields, the sounds of the cattle moving, their animalness, their mass, their thudding hooves—and our ultimate success—was an experience to remember, really "cool" as our granddaughter Monique would say. How jarring it then was to see the trucker and his helper in the barnyard beating the cattle with 2x4s to get them up the ramp into the truck.

Our career as beef farmers ended abruptly. That fall, local full-time beef farmers who knew what they were doing, experienced losses of $100 a head, so low were the prices. We were lucky. Our cattle had gained more than usual, about 300 pounds each in the short time they had been on our fields. Even though two had died, our revenue from selling the survivors equalled our costs and direct expenses. While it's fun to do different things, it's not fun to lose money. We have stayed out of the beef business ever since.

One of the disconcerting things about the marketplace is how irrational it is. Cattle are sold on the hoof by the pound. In the spring, farmers buy cattle (spring feeders) weighing upwards of 500 pounds, for about $1.10 per pound or more. In the fall, after six months of suffering the slings and arrows of everyday farming—after he has trucked the cattle, fed them, medicated them, chased them and fenced them—the farmer will be able to sell them for anywhere between 65-85 cents per pound. Obviously, the only way the farmer can break even is to have cattle that have gained a lot, well above average.

On second thought, it's not the market, but the farmer who must be irrational to continue farming. Will Canadian farmers ever become so "rational" that no wheat will be harvested? No livestock produced? No dairy herds milked? No cheese made? No eggs laid? No vegetables grown?

So, AS CAUTIOUS, risk-averse farmers, we decided to focus on improving our pasture, but even that reinforced what we already knew and what so many city dwellers do not. Farming costs money and requires labour. After getting rid of at least some of the old fence-rows, after burning off the dead elms, after removing hawthorns, after stone-picking, after bulldozing out huge boulders which had been left in mid-field, after re-building the barn, we ended up with fields that had not been fertilized for years. They had been thoroughly depleted by cattle grazing summer after summer.

Norm wasn't farming anymore, so we reached an agreement with a young farmer who was cheery, robust and optimistic. Alec Robertson was still living with his mother and ran her farm just up the fifth line. The Fifth Line Schoolhouse from which we had rescued wainscotting for our kitchen counter, had been built on a corner of the Robertson property. Alec helped on his brother Dave's dairy farm. He also "worked out." City types may think working out means aerobic exercises in a gym. Here in Sydenham, farmers who "work out" have a job in town. On top of everything else, Alec partied hard.

Alec agreed to plough and plant trefoil. Fertilizer is expensive and so is seed. The fields did get ploughed—but the way Alec ploughed them must be unique in the annals of farming. Late one evening we heard the sound of his tractor. Visibility was good because there was a bright full moon, but in addition to the moonlight, Alec had the tractor's headlights on full beam. We watched, astonished. There was Alec, riding his huge, new, green tractor like a knight on a charger galloping into battle. He zoomed over the fields. The tractor leapt into the air, crashed down and then up it went again. The field got ploughed in record time and Alec didn't fall off. How long the tractor endured this kind of life I don't know, but Alec most definitely got our fields ploughed. And grain was seeded, under-planted with trefoil.

Don Emmerson then took over from Alec. He put 20 cattle out to graze, took as many as 3000 bales of hay off our fields, and planted grain for several years, taking off 12 tons one year. Now Don uses all our fields for hay, and our barn to store it. The yield is diminishing because the fields need fertilizing. That's for the next ten-year plan.

WE REMAINED convinced that farming means animals. So when we found ourselves with like-minded people to the south and to the north of us, we began a new career as chicken farmers. At this time Janos and Lou still owned the Eddy Morrison farm next door and were renting it to a colleague of mine, Derek Cassels, then editor of a Toronto-based national medical publication. With two sons, and an assortment of other people, Derek's extended family was enjoying their weekend retreat as much as we enjoyed ours. Meantime to the north, another friend, Philip Downs had bought Norm Smith's old farm, the place where Speely Morrison so long ago had tried to hide his family's farm equipment to prevent it from being sold off at the bankruptcy auction. Ever since Andrew and Philip had met in the six-ties while completing their PhDs at the University of Toronto's Massey College, we had been friends with Philip and his family. Philip was a musicologist and gifted musician. While he owned his farm, we spent many hours making music with him at the Hougues Magues. But Philip, like Janos, would sell his farm after just a few years.

The three families decided to form a chicken cooperative. It was only possible to contemplate such a scheme because Derek's compan-ion Rose was spending the whole summer at the farm. She was pre-pared to look after the chickens during the week and the rest of us would take over on weekends. We bought several dozen chicks, spent a fortune on feed, and very quickly learned just how stupid chickens are. Once past chickhood, chickens are not at all endearing. When there was a storm they all piled into a corner and suffocated those wit-less enough to be at the bottom of the pile. Those who escaped suffo-cation were left for raccoons and foxes to dine on at night in spite of our best efforts at fortification.

By fall, it was time to slaughter those that remained. Philip and Andrew were determined we should do it ourselves, finishing what you start and all that. Andrew was to pith them (i.e., pierce or sever the spinal cord) expertly while Philip held them in the right position for the sacrificial act. I would pluck the feathers and Andrew was prepared to gut them. What a mess! The gore and squawking were bad enough, but it took forever to pluck them, even though the theory was that a correct mode of killing guaranteed that the feathers would come off easily. The feathers flew all over us and everywhere else. After we had done about half a dozen, we accepted defeat. The rest of the chickens were taken to the Mennonites. For a small charge, they did everything necessary to prepare the birds for the freezer. Probably the best chickens we have ever eaten. Chicken farmers we were, but one summer was enough.

⁕

OUR CURRENT arrangement, focusing on hay and trees, seems ideal for weekend farmers. The land is much improved since we came. And we have learned quite a bit about farming!

Chapter 15

How Did Our Garden Grow?

We all must cultivate our gardens.

Voltaire's *Candide*.

⟨━━⟨⟩━━⟩

GARDENING WAS NOT one of our things back in 1971. Uninformed and relatively uninterested would fairly describe us then, with respect to gardens, although we did enjoy looking at them. One more example of how much the farm has changed us. Now we have visited gardens in Canada, England, France, Italy and Japan. Long before it was fashionable, Andrew became obsessed with gardening. He now has bookshelves of gardening books and has acquired a new vocabulary.

Looking back, Andrew agrees with me that our first preoccupation was to establish a windbreak at the perimeter of the garden. The prevailing wind is from the southwest which was undoubtedly why the mortar kept falling out of the south walls. With the exception of a few small cedars on the north, four old honey locusts near the house, and the dying elm trees on the fence-rows, the fields and hills around us were forlornly bare. The wind swept up our small valley driving rain through the loose mortar, lifting the loose shingles from the roof and depositing them onto the lawn, rattling the windows and making us shiver with the drafts.

House, old barn and lane c. 1973. Lawn is ready for seeding.

Having attended night classes run by the University of Guelph on woodlot management, we had lots of information about windbreaks. The general principle was to plant up to three rows of trees, with one row planted in quick-growing trees, the other two in slow growers. The quick growers were poplars. The slow growers we planted included Austrian pine, cedar, and because my father adored them, blue spruce. That triple planting protected the house on the south and west. A hedge of cedars extended the western facade of the house southwards because we wanted to create a horizontal sweep to what was at that time a starkly vertical house. (That hedge also gives us privacy when strangers drive up.) Cedars and spruce were planted to the north to protect us from north winds.

Many years later, what has happened? Trees now enclose the house and shade the vegetable garden, stunting growth. The inevitable remedy of course has been to cut down some trees close to the house. Some cedars have been sacrificed but Michael and Nickie salvaged their flexible branches to make an attractive rustic garden chair, so the cedar's spirit remains. The poplars are another story. As they grew taller they threatened our electric power lines which is why Ben Redmond felled six of them.

Whatever benefit accrues from the satisfyingly quick growth of poplars and their elegant shape has to be weighed against their numerous disadvantages. In storms they are fragile—twigs and branches are torn off and litter the lawn far and wide. There is always the risk, when they get very tall, that the trees will snap. They are profligate with suckers, so if you want a tree-like conformation rather than a bush, pruning is required every spring. Now to be fair, a whole lot of trees need pruning, not just poplars. However, all the poplar's disadvantages are trivial compared to what happens when you cut one down. A poplar's will to live is fearsome—when you cut it down, innocently believing that you have rid yourself of it, the poplar has other intentions. Within weeks, if not days, small poplar shoots can be seen sprouting up in the garden and in the adjacent fields, sometimes at a distance of 30 and 40 feet. And the stump itself sends up dozens of shoots. Cutting down poplars requires measures similar to those we had used with the hawthorns. Roundup must be poured into a hole drilled into the freshly cut stump to discourage unwanted re-growth.

As for the honey locusts that now stand within the garden boundaries, they have their disadvantages too. They are the last tree to come into leaf in the spring, probably because they are indigenous to the U.S. South and keep waiting for warmer weather. In the fall, they drop hard, dark brown pods about 12 inches long, all over the lawn and driveway. Worst of all, they have piercing thorns, up to 3 inches long and sharp as sharp. When they prick you, you're guaranteed to be sore at the puncture site for the next several days. However, these trees have an interesting story. About 100 years ago, a salesman from the U.S. came to Grey County, advertising in newspapers (we've seen the ads) that he was selling a "living fence." The idea was that with their long thorns, these trees if planted close together would be effective barriers to all living beings forever. Many of them still survive, thorns at the ready to attack whomever approaches. Fences they are not.

THE VEGETABLE GARDEN was our next preoccupation. Andrew tilled and fertilized a large vegetable patch behind the house. In full sun from early mid-morning on, it flourished. We spent the whole month of July at the Hougues Magues during the children's holidays, so during this crucial month the garden was regularly weeded and watered. The result was we had an abundance of delicious vegetables, enjoying as many as four or five different kinds at one meal.

In the first years, we weren't bothered by unwelcome visitors coming to eat our crop when we weren't looking. Things gradually changed. As the children grew older, we divided our holidays—two weeks at the farm in August and two weeks travelling at other times of the year. Less attention to vegetables, then fewer vegetables, and then a smaller vegetable patch was the result. Worse, with reforestation and improved habitat, wildlife increased dramatically and so did visits to the garden by nibbling animals. One day while Andrew was weeding, he looked up to see a rabbit beside him, boldly dining on our lettuce. The groundhogs had been nuisance enough. The rabbit was the last straw. Andrew built Fort Groundhog.

He made a raised bed, about 4x10 feet, with cedar logs and then filled it with soil and compost. He surmounted it with a rectangular cage of chicken wire. Three sides of the cage—two short and one long—were fixed to the cedar frame rising to about 4 feet above ground level. The roof of the cage and the remaining long side were joined by hinges, while more hinges joined the roof to the fixed wall of the cage. By this means Andrew could raise the roof (and one hinged side) to tend his lettuce, spinach, arugula and basil. When he was finished, roof and wall were lowered and fastened, and fauna in search of a feast were frustrated. But so was Andrew, because it's very difficult to reach the back of the bed and the roof is very heavy. Better ways must be devised.

The trees we planted on the hill behind the house have kept on growing taller and taller and the garden is getting fewer and fewer hours of sun. Now as we look at a very skimpy yield from what remains of the vegetable garden, the future becomes obvious. The vegetable patch will be moved soon to the sunny fields south of the house. A true experimental scientist, Andrew in 1999 stuck one tomato plant in the field. No attention, no water, no mulch, no protection. It flourished in comparison to its siblings in the sun-starved garden.

THEN CAME THE HOUSE GARDEN. The Millers had built a rail fence around the house, but the area they had enclosed was long and very narrow and the south fence was very close to the house. (I can remember hearing cows chomping and breathing heavily just outside our bedroom window early one morning when Norm's cattle were still here. It sounded as though they were actually in our bedroom.) We wanted a wider garden, one which did not go quite as far west as the Miller's. Moving the fence meant we had to convert some field to lawn. Smoothing and preparing the soil for seeding was a major effort, especially when the topsoil we ordered was full of garbage—bits of plastic, tin cans and glass—which we had to remove, but the end result has been a lawn that is good enough to please us.

The first flowers we paid attention to were the peonies, already in the garden when we came, and daffodils. We moved the peonies from one place to another trying to find the "best" spot for them without any regard to what their needs were, an experience which the peonies did not particularly appreciate. To punish us, they stopped blooming for several years. The daffodils given to us by my Uncle Theo, reappear joyously every spring. Now they bloom not only in their original bed, but all over the garden and even around our new pond.

One summer we visited Manfred's Garden near Craigleith, a beautifully landscaped retail outlet. That visit led to Andrew's ultimate addiction to gardening, an addiction which becomes more absorbing each year. Manfred's Garden was imaginatively designed and the plants for sale were much more interesting than the petunias and pansies which prevailed at the time. Andrew returned to the farm and immediately set about building his first rockery. I think it was then that we decided to disdain annuals and go for perennials in the mistaken belief they would be less work. In any case, Andrew remembers that my mother instantly approved of the rockery, and I disapproved. My only excuse would have been that new projects meant less time for existing ones—and that has not changed to this day.

The Hougues Magues is situated on a marked slope which rises from west to east quite sharply behind the house. Eventually Andrew realized that slopes are anathema to gardeners. Terracing was the answer. Our first terrace was built up at the front of the house. The ground level needed to be raised to make the house look as though it was planted in, rather than perched on, the land. After a nice flat area had been created in front of the house, curving around the corner to the old apple tree, we needed steps to descend to the driveway. The first steps were railway ties, but later when we put in a patio outside the kitchen, the railway ties were replaced with patio bricks.

More terraces soon followed. One was made simply by extending the first small rockery. The second one demanded to be made urgently when the verandah was being built on the north side of the house. Quite in contrast to the front, the rear of the house needed the ground level to be lowered. It was at least two feet too high, coming quite close to the sill of the back kitchen window. The verandah's foundation began at a level at least five feet below the natural ground level. After the excavation for the foundation had been completed, not only did we need to remedy an ugly and unwelcome mud-hole, but we also had to deal with water that was seeping out of the side of the well behind the house—the same well that a young visitor had fallen into so many years ago.

In a single day, Michael and Andrew, knee-deep in watery mud and using stones they had wheel-barrowed over from the fence-rows, constructed five steps rising from what would be the new and much

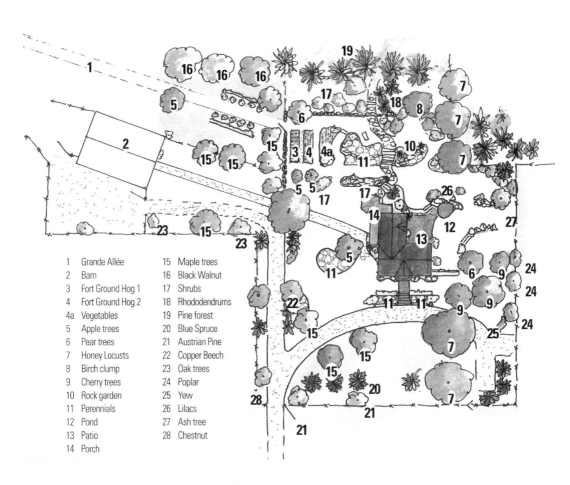

Andrew's Garden Plan.

1	Grande Allée	15	Maple trees
2	Barn	16	Black Walnut
3	Fort Ground Hog 1	17	Shrubs
4	Fort Ground Hog 2	18	Rhododendrums
4a	Vegetables	19	Pine forest
5	Apple trees	20	Blue Spruce
6	Pear trees	21	Austrian Pine
7	Honey Locusts	22	Copper Beech
8	Birch clump	23	Oak trees
9	Cherry trees	24	Poplar
10	Rock garden	25	Yew
11	Perennials	26	Lilacs
12	Pond	27	Ash tree
13	Patio	28	Chestnut
14	Porch		

lower level of the lawn surrounding the verandah. The steps emerged miraculously quickly in what truly had been a disaster area. Once the steps were completed Andrew built a rockery on either side of them, and before long there were three terraces separated by two rockeries to the rear of the house.

Rockeries also flanked both sides of the front steps. Separated from the lawn above by a low hedge of pink-flowering spirea, these two rockeries display peonies and iris beautifully in the spring and roses, purple sage, speedwell, baby's breath, artemesia, Scotch thistle and lilies in the summer. But what the garden still lacked were flowerbeds.

There was the bed close to the drive as it enters the garden, where Uncle Theo's daffodils were first planted. This bed exists only in the spring and then is covered in grass. Three new flowerbeds were developed. A relatively small one is across the driveway from the daffodil bed. Its main glory is phlox, day lilies, Russian sage, grasses and a Victorian gazing globe. Another small bed with phlox, a pin cherry, grasses, lamb's tongues, hosta, gentian, day lilies and a sundial, is close to the parking area in front of the house. The largest bed, kidney shaped, curving around the apple tree, is filled with bluebells, peonies, iris, tall grasses, lady's mantle, foxglove, pulmonaria, bleeding heart, grasses, sea holly, delphiniums, day lilies, lilies, sedums and fall anemones.

Over the years we have learned that there are plants as well as trees that are wisely avoided. The first was borage. Its exuberant growth was initially irresistible. We soon changed our minds. It spreads and is very hard to get rid of. The same is true for goutweed, a ground cover that will not be stopped, and is impossible to discourage. I've taken a dislike to lamb's ears, not because it is unattractive, but because it sends forth volunteers everywhere, precisely where you don't want them and it smothers less rambunctious plants. Soapwort is bad for the same reason and so is mint which should only be grown in a pot. Finally we have a type of oregano which invades mercilessly and has to be pulled up spring after spring after spring. Don't be tempted by quick growth.

For many years we had made no use of the really large rocks that dotted our fields and dominated our fence-rows. A trip to Japan changed all that. Once Andrew had seen how Japanese gardeners used rocks, greenery and water, he was truly inspired. On returning to the Hougues Magues, he chose eight or nine huge boulders to bring to the garden. Then he hired a large front-end loader, leading the driver to one fence row after another, to remove the rocks he had chosen. Once these large rocks were brought to the garden, Andrew knew precisely where each was to be placed, how deep, which end would be up, and at what angle. Those he selected are remarkable in complexity, shape, striations and colour. As a result, the sloping land south of the house now has three levels. The upper one joins with the terrace behind the house. The middle one, continuous with the brick kitchen patio, is excellent for playing croquet. And the lowest terrace, a shady nook with a cherry tree and a pear tree, is a pleasant refuge on hot summer days.

The final touch was the placement of several large boulders to form a backdrop for a small lily pond beside the kitchen patio. Multitudes of frogs, large and small, have taken up residence in this little pond. Ignoring the grass blades noisily showered on their habitat when the lawn is mowed, they occupy their lily pads and perch on small stone ledges, fascinating both young and old.

Andrew's most recent project in the garden is a "Grande Allée" extending northward behind the barn. An avenue of grass, it is bordered by wild apple trees and cedars, lilies and forsythia, with a small statue at its far end. It is there to be discovered, a nice surprise. Most visitors never notice it.

❧❦❧

TENDING OUR GARDEN is a constant challenge. Too often we travel in the late spring, a time when a garden really needs a lot of attention. Even our regular routine, being away for just five days most weeks is a disadvantage. Keeping up with weeding is impossible. Water shortages are always a problem although installing a cistern to collect rainwater from the barn roof has been a great help. Year after year, flowering annuals in our planters were more often wilted than not. Then in

1999 we filled our planters with varieties of sedum that thrive even when we are not around to water them. They have been a great success.

Birds can also be a problem: nuthatches brutally attacked two birch trees planted in memory of Andrew's father. Then we discovered Tanglefoot, and it successfully kept the nuthatches off the trees. Always challenges, and usually solutions.

That summarizes how our garden grew. Planting details are shown in Andrew's diagram of the garden, but the garden changes from one year to the next. In 1999, Andrew concentrated on bringing more light and shape into the forest which now threatens to smother the house from behind. Because of close spacing, the trees—cedar, spruce, pine, maple and ash—lose their individuality. Their shape, texture and colour have condensed into an oppressive, homogeneous mass. At lunch today we discussed which trees should be sacrificed. I can already hear the chainsaw. It's easier to fell trees than to clean them up. We will definitely be renting the big chipper.

Chapter 16

Gilding the Lily

Permissible pleasure or compulsive disorder?

Entry from my diary, July 22, 1993

1979 WAS NOT ONLY the year of cattle problems. It was also the year of major furnace disasters. The furnace problems would never have arisen if we had lived full time at the farm. But we could not and did not. Our choice was to be frugal with fuel and to turn down the thermostat every time we left the farm. That had inevitable and undesirable consequences. Because it was set at 8°C, the chimney cooled down. Hot air rose only intermittently from the furnace so moisture condensed high in the chimney and water fell back into the furnace. Over time, the firebox rusted out.

In March, 1979 we still did not realize what was going on in the chimney. I wrote in the farm diary: *It is four weeks ago tonight that we were last here on which occasion we departed the house at approximately 3 a.m. We had noticed a slight odour of fuel oil on going to bed but Andrew found a leak in the oil line, reported it to the plumber who had installed the furnace eight years ago, and was assured all was well. By 2:30 Nigel was awakened by our smoke detector and called us all. The house was filled with black smoke which burned in our chests. After Andrew turned off the furnace, we all returned to our beds. After four or five minutes I declared that inhaling that air for another four hours would be intolerable. Out we went into the cold, 30 below it was said. The car of course would not start in such cold, so we walked over to the McKibbons who were still up at 3:30 a.m. We slept for a few hours in their kitchen and then drove home without returning to the farm.*

The house to which we have returned (4 weeks later) is a sorry mess. Within moments of entering one's hands are gray. Black cobwebs dangle from the ceiling. A delicate powder of soot lies on furniture, appliances, sinks and floors. You can wipe something clean and within minutes it's dirty because, in spite of the service call, the furnace continues to circulate soot.

In fact it would be a month before the service people recognized that the furnace needed to be replaced. We remained ignorant of the underlying cause and blithely installed a second oil furnace. We mistakenly assumed that we had finally found a knowledgeable serviceman. By May, when we started having our problems with the cattle, the house was just about getting back to normal after all the painting and cleaning. This was *not* gilding the lily. It was just restoring the house to its previous state. We were grateful our insurance covered our expenses.

When the second furnace also rusted out—a situation we recognized before we had another smoky episode, no heating expert we consulted offered any explanation. But Andrew on his own deduced the underlying mechanism. Furnace number three is electric. No more worries about fuel delivery in the middle of the winter. No opportunity for the furnace to rust out, at least so far. No need for a chimney.

In the meantime, both Nickie and I were doing Master's degrees at McMaster University in Hamilton, Ontario. Although she was in the Faculty of Engineering and I in Medicine, we were often able to meet for lunch, a pair of graduate students who happened to be mother and daughter. June, 1980 was a busy month. I defended my thesis, Nickie married Michael, and Andrew, Nigel and I left for a year in Oxford, England. The newlyweds moved into our Toronto house and managed the farm. When we returned, I switched from part-time to full-time employment. We could now spend more money on the farm.

❦

THREE DAYS BEFORE I started writing this book, while taking a first-time guest to her bedroom, I said that the upstairs hall had just had its first coat of green paint, and that the next time she came, it would have had its second coat and Andrew would have put up crown moulding. Her response was, "You are house-proud, aren't you?" It's not the first time I have considered this notion. Back in 1993 I wrote in my diary: *I have so much pleasure in improving our two homes with Andrew, but I am not always sure whether it is a permissible pleasure or a compulsive disorder. Witold Rybczynski in his book* Home: a Short History of an Idea *makes a wonderful case that it is a very human activity and an important one. The home is an organic being rather than a container for materialism and its products. Rybczynski describes the homes of some famous people, like Robert Louis Stevenson and Mark Twain. Twain felt his home responded to his presence. Which parallels my feeling that the Hougues Magues withdraws from us about two hours before we leave it, although that doesn't happen with the house in Toronto.*

I am convinced that there are dead homes and living homes. Dead homes are what you see so often in interior decorating magazines. Inevitably these are very expensive homes. The rooms often have been created at one point in time, clearly signalling that they are the work of a designer. They have not evolved over the years to reveal layers of the owners' life experiences and history. Instead these rooms are usually predictably and fashionably contrived. It is the owners of such rooms who are house-proud, because for them, their house is an important symbol indicating to others their affluent status, rather than a place for their own comfort and joy. There is another kind of dead home, lived in by people at the end of their lives when they don't really care about their surroundings, and don't want to spend time or money to re-awaken their dwelling.

Janos Hrabovszky, now in his seventies, continues to make and restore fine furniture as his retirement hobby. A long time ago, I asked him how looking after *things* could ever be justified when there were always *people* to care for. His reply was that people made beautiful things in the past, and respect for those people requires that we continue now to look after what they made. I think a living home reflects respect for the people who made its contents, the people who gave any of the contents, and the people who live within. When a home is made esthetically pleasing, it becomes a place where people can find solace, comfort and pleasure. Advocates of grunge can disagree.

Living homes by nature change from month to month, as opportunities are taken to rearrange objects or to improve what is already there by upholstering, painting or refinishing. All this requires mental effort, as anyone who has tried to hang their pictures for best effect will know. I'm not talking about new pictures and new furniture. So in response to my houseguest, The Hougues Magues is alive and Andrew and I enjoy interacting with it.

⁂

BUILDING A VERANDAH in 1985 proved an ambitious project. Up until that time, if we wanted to sit outdoors at the farm, we either sat under the apple tree, or out on the brick kitchen patio—but both places left us unprotected from insects and the furniture unprotected from rain. The verandah we designed had its roots in Lakefield and in Stratford, two charming Ontario towns.

Andrew's aunt and uncle, Kate and Kim Krenz, had a turn-of-the-century brick house in Lakefield. When we visited them, I was always struck by their verandah and the variety of ways it could be used. One third of it was glassed in and could be used for meals even on cool days in early spring and late fall. One third was screened in, floor to ceiling, and offered protection even while outdoors. The third part was unscreened and open, sheltered only by the roof. That was the Lakefield example.

As for Stratford, it hosts the Stratford Festival which is why we are there every summer. Thanks to a prosperous railway industry in times past, Stratford has many elegant homes. What caught my eye were the columned brick verandahs. Often extending along two sides of a house, they had pod-like extensions and hexagonal conical roofs at the point where they made their right-angled turns around the corner of the houses. It was an idea worth repeating.

Before long, I had designed our new porch. Like Kate and Kim's, it had a glassed-in section, relatively small, which provided a sheltered winter entrance. The remainder was to be screened in. Like Stratford verandahs, it had an octagonal pod extending from the corner which provided a room-like space. When the rest of the family saw the plan, they feared that the verandah roof would diminish the view from the kitchen and make it darker. They were right. But the sacrifice was accepted, we went ahead, and everyone has enjoyed the verandah ever since.

The verandah was built with some hiccups. The first surprise was a moat of mud and water around the newly poured cement foundation. Water was seeping out of the exposed side of the well behind the house. Worse, the workers had severed the water line connecting the spring to the house. Because our basement pump sucked the muddy water into our water storage tank, we had dirt in our water for the next year. A more serious problem was that the foundation for the octagonal pod was slightly asymmetrical due to less-than-meticulous measuring when the forms for the concrete were being made. It required a very skilled carpenter to make the frame for the roof under these circumstances. Then the contractor had problems getting custom doors, windows and screens made. The upshot was that the doors and windows he installed were not made of properly aged wood and so they have warped. And we never did get the gingerbread corners for the screen panels we had hoped for.

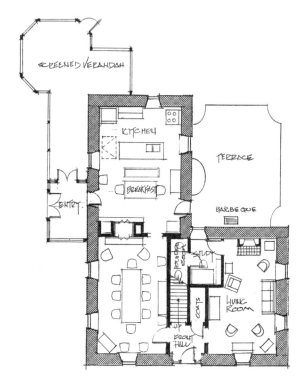

1st Floor

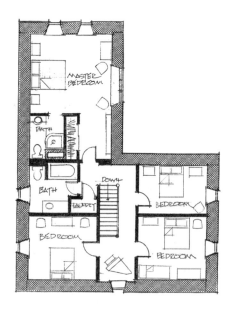

2nd Floor

1995 House layout.

Drawn by George Yost.

184

As often happened, a change in our Toronto home precipitated change at the Hougues Magues. In 1990 major renovations to our Toronto kitchen displaced an old pine cupboard. Its new home had to be the farm kitchen—but only after some changes were made. We put the cupboard where the stove had previously been and the stove was shifted to where the chimney cupboard had been. Then, above the stove we built new kitchen cabinets.

Cabinet doors must inspire our creativity. This time, instead of using the upper thirds of old doors as we had for the island counter, we used some old gothic-paned windows we had stashed away. We stripped and varnished the pine frames, put in new glass, and stretched gathered white sheers on the inside. We think they look great.

⁕⁕⁕

My mother's move in 1994 from a large apartment into a small one set off more major changes at the Hougues Magues. These changes all catapulted from her dining-room suite. My mother was very attached to her solid oak Jacobean-style dining-room furniture. She and my father had purchased it during the Depression, probably at an auction, and she always claimed it had been custom-made for a Rosedale stockbroker who had gone bankrupt. (Rosedale is an enclave where the wealthiest of Torontonians have long chosen to live.) I can remember when the high-backed, cowhide-covered chairs were taller than me, when moving them required all my strength, and when the space underneath the table, sectored into four triangles by the cross boards close to the floor, was my private domain.

My mother was upset enough about leaving her big apartment; to upset her further by selling her dining-room suite was impossible. Andrew, who didn't particularly like 20th century Jacobean oak, was not thrilled when I suggested it move to the farm. Not for the first time, he allowed me to persuade him to proceed with a project that he wasn't sure he would like.

Some project! Up until then, the kitchen at the Hougues Magues had also served as our dining-room. My mother's furniture couldn't go in the kitchen because there wasn't enough space. It needed a room of its own. What happened? Her dining-room furniture took over our living-room, our living-room moved into our main-floor bedroom and our bedroom had to be moved upstairs to the playroom. The former main floor *en suite* bathroom was sectored into a powder room and a small study for Andrew, the kitchen enjoyed some refurbishment, and new homes were found for articles which had been in the playroom. Once started, why stop? So even more was done. The second floor bathroom acquired an attractive new floor, new ceramic tiles replaced tile board around the tub enclosure, and an exhaust fan was installed. And fresh wallpaper.

Indeed, some aspects of this cascade of change were easily accomplished. Instantly transformed were the kitchen and the new dining-room. Our pine kitchen benefited enormously from the removal of the undistinguished second-hand walnut-stained dining-room set we had used for so long. My mother's dining-room furniture suited extraordinarily well our previous living-room with its pale gray-green walls and white-painted woodwork. It all looked comfortably elegant. Sadly, Oma would only ever see photographs.

The transformation of our downstairs bedroom into a living-room was less satisfactory. The furniture worked, but the wallpaper, chosen for a bedroom, was not ideal for a living-room. But with all the changes that were necessary upstairs to convert the playroom into our bedroom, we were quite content to leave the living-room wallpaper until later.

The playroom was long and low-ceilinged. At its far end were the original two windows, rather small and with pine sills and plaster reveals. It had always been a very dark room. The changes we wanted were simple and straightforward, however effecting them was not. We decided to raise the ceiling so there would be no attic, just the A-shape of the original roof. We also decided to install a large casement window in the south wall, the window we like to look out of in the morning while we drink our coffee in bed. We also needed a new floor. After that, all we needed were bookshelves, a clothes closet, and a tiny three-piece bathroom with a skylight. It was all done—including repairing the kitchen ceiling and upgrading the guest bathroom—in about two months.

But time has passed since then and more has been done. The new living-room lacked what the old one had enjoyed, namely a fireplace —it was enough to make the rest of the family complain bitterly whenever we sat there. I was not enthusiastic about carrying firewood in and ashes out through the house. There was enough mess with the existing wood fireplace. Andrew agreed it was a good idea to have a fireplace that would provide instant gratification with no work required, neither chopping nor hauling. So at the same time that we installed a propane stove in the kitchen guaranteeing hot food when the power was off, we also installed a propane fireplace in the new living room guaranteeing a second source of heat. Andrew built the mantel surround using local Eramosa marble and pine, both salvaged and new. For the hearth, he used slate tiles left over from our Toronto kitchen floor. For above the mantle shelf, Andrew used old pine to frame a large mirror. Most of our visitors think we have a "real" fireplace once it's lit, but our children remain mildly disapproving.

CLUSTER FLIES routinely made windows and windowsills filthy, until the house was regularly sprayed. For most of our years at the farm, cleaning the windows, aluminum storms on the outside and the old sash windows inside, was a dreaded task keeping me busy for days. I had to unscrew the narrow window-stripping that held in place the lower half of the sash window. The window could then be removed and washed. Every crevice and every corner in the sill would be jammed with fly carcasses. Next, and always a struggle, the screen and storm window had to be removed for cleaning. The grooves of their frames would be packed with fly fragments, which all had to be pried out with a knife. Cleaning the exterior of the upper half of the sash window was best done from outside—which meant ladders, and Andrew did that.

It took far too much time to remove, clean and reassemble all the windows. Furthermore, the reluctance of old sash windows to open more than a few inches, or to open at all, was a constant irritation. In contrast, the modern screens and double-glazed casement windows in our new bedroom were a joy. They could be opened only a fraction for fresh air in the winter, or full out at a 90° angle to the sill, letting fresh air in unhindered in the summer. Best of all, I could sit on the sill and wash them in minutes, inside and out, quite effortlessly. All these advantages were irresistible. So new casement windows were installed in all the second floor windows. Guests who remember what it was like in the past, report the bedrooms are much warmer in the winter. I'm not sure they notice the windows are cleaner, but they certainly appreciate the absence of flies.

THERE IS ALWAYS something else to do. In 1998, we finally decided we couldn't stand the old bedroom wallpaper in our new living-room. The paper was now over twenty years old. Do manufacturers deliberately mislead their customers with false promises? A "dry-strippable" wallpaper? What a joke! It's dry-strippable, but only partially. The patterned upper layer can be stripped off with no effort at all. The under-layer isn't even wet-strippable although the manufacturer's instructions for hanging wallpaper (preparation with tri-sodium phosphate and then wall-sizing) had been followed meticulously. In spite of the reluctance of the paper to leave the walls, we managed eventually to completely rid them of both old paper and old paste. Then holes and cracks were patched. And crown moulding? With crown molding we were getting really fancy, but an example had been set. It simply could not be ignored.

Torontonians George Yost and Kathy Lochnan own a stone house in North Sydenham similar to ours. They've not owned it as long as we have owned the Hougues Magues, but they have accomplished miracles in their house. George, trained in architecture, is a do-it-yourselfer sans pareil (after Andrew, that is!). He was the one who showed me how to handle angles when putting up wallpaper borders in rooms with sloping ceilings, and who persuaded me it was quite possible to use large-patterned wallpaper in small spaces. He was the one who cajoled me into taking evening courses in upholstery at George Brown Community College in Toronto where he was a regular attender. This led to my upholstering seven Toronto dining-room chairs and another nine chairs at the farm as well as repairing two antique chairs. A trickle-down effect followed when Nickie decided to take the course too.

But that was not the end of George's inspiring example. After Andrew and I saw the crown moulding George had installed in their living-room, we were determined to emulate him. As George says, crown moulding "finishes off" a room, particularly rooms with high ceilings. With crown moulding selling for 45 cents a foot at Home Depot and Bea Glazebrook living just around the corner from us at the farm, yet another project began. Bea is a cabinet-maker and had the mitre necessary to make the seven inside and four outside corners that our living-room needed. She and I spent several days together, at the end of which our new living-room was adorned with crown moulding, most satisfying to behold.

Next step—choosing wallpaper. As far as I'm concerned, to choose wallpaper is to suffer the tortures of the damned. Not only is it difficult to find what you think you want, you also have to get family consensus. With pine, we have decided, there are only three colour choices—blue, green or white, although George has used pale yellow very successfully. Ultimately we chose a dark blue mottled pattern, blue because it complemented our rug and furniture. Unlike the rest of the family, I had grave misgivings before hanging it, but combined with the crown moulding and a matching border, our new look is definitely a success.

As I write, we are in the midst of more dirt and chaos. The antique-white upstairs hall and stairwell have not been painted since the early seventies. New wallpaper in the entrance vestibule chosen specifically to be a transition between the green dining-room and the blue living-room, nudged us into repainting the upstairs hall. This time we chose dark green. In the spring of 1999, Nickie and I put on the first coat to see if we liked living with it. It set off the pine superbly.

Crown moulding having caught our fancy, we decided we wanted it in the upstairs hall too. George, ever helpful, explained how to deal with moulding when you have sloping ceilings. This time it was Andrew who installed the moulding, undaunted by a ceiling that is one inch higher on one side of the narrow hall than the other. He even put up a ceiling rosette. Then it was time for me to put two coats of white paint on the ceiling, the moulding and the plaster window reveals and a second coat of green paint on the walls.

That we could do all this in spite of an intimidating 20-foot stairwell, is because of good advice from Bert Seupersaud. Anyone wanting to paint a stairwell may benefit, provided the top of their stairwell is bordered by handrail and ballisters on one side and one end. He told us to place a stepladder on the floor at the top of the stairs, and to position a long, wide plank so that it extends from the second or third step of the ladder, across the long axis of the stairwell to the top of the handrail opposite the ladder. Then to place a second plank on top of the first so that it goes angle-wise from the ladder to the handrail on the side of the stairwell. Finally to place a third plank, going from the middle of the side handrail to the middle of the end handrail, overlapping the ends of the first two planks and completing a triangle. Stand on it carefully. It bounces.

One more task before the hall could be completely finished. Buy clear pine moulding, stain it so that it matched the old pine and use it as surrounds for the door and window frames. Job done. Much satisfaction. Angus McArthur would be astonished and might well consider it a waste of time and money.

Next will be crown moulding in the dining-room. There is one more door that needs stripping upstairs. The kitchen needs a new floor. Always more furniture to refinish. Perhaps we need more bedrooms for more grandchildren? The best homes grow.

❦

CHANGES ON THE LAND? We decided we would like a pond closer to the house, away from the beavers—a smaller pond because that was all that the land would permit. The site we chose was in a hollow, to the left of where the lane beyond the barn turns to go up the hill. Just as we had before, we consulted the ministry for a plan. We were permitted once again to dam the creek but this time we were told that the overflow must draw from the bottom of the pond. A high-hoe was brought in and the creek bed was widened and excavated. A choice boulder was selected for the convenience of divers. For the benefit of people who do not like diving, Andrew has to build a new dock. Because the pond is quite small, landscaping—trees, bulrushes, water lilies—was soon accomplished. Best of all, it only takes five minutes to walk there from the house. We are regularly welcomed by frogs of all sizes and occasionally by one very large turtle.

More fencing is always needed. The last major tree-planting by the ministry occurred in the spring of 1981 while we were in England on sabbatical. Very reluctantly we had decided to have larches planted on the slopes we had originally wanted to keep for hay. The slopes made cutting hay just too difficult, even dangerous. But planting more trees meant building more fences and build them we did. In the early nineties, yet another government grant became available. This time the ministry wanted fences to be installed to protect watercourses from being damaged by livestock. Cattle break down the banks of creeks and rivers to reach the water. Mud is stirred up from the bottom, there is fecal contamination and erosion is accelerated. Because our creek flowed into the Bighead River, we were eligible for this new grant. We put up rail fences on both sides of our creek.

More gravel is always needed. Gravel for a lane one-half kilometre long. Gravel for the barnyard. Gravel delivered when you are not there. Careless truckers who dump the gravel too quickly so all the gravel is used up in a place where you really didn't need it. Frustrations!

We must improve the pasture before too long. The trees need thinning and that will mean some income from our managed forest.

Lots of things to do.

Chapter 17

Parties to Remember

*There were twelve, very large, cold rice puddings with an abundance
of currants in them, the same number of bun loaves with eight or
nine dozen of both ginger-bread cakes and of currant cakes and plenty
of bread and butter. In the meat line there was lamb and poultry.*

Letter from Anne Langton, July 23, 1842.

THERE ARE DIFFERENT KINDS of parties. There are those that provide an opportunity to be seen rubbing shoulders with important people, immediately establishing of course that everyone
who attends is important. Such parties can be entertaining, and sometimes the food is excellent. Other parties are primarily an occasion for
showing the company flag, or perhaps displaying commitment to a
good cause. They can be fun too. Finally there are parties that are
designed to do none of the above. They focus on friends who like each
other enough that showing off isn't necessary; friends who tolerate you
even when you are objectionable. That third kind of party is definitely
a Hougues Magues kind of party.

    The fact that Andrew and I host some big parties is not quite
consistent with our usual preference to entertain no more that four to
six people at a time—which is what we mostly do. But on special occasions, preparing for big parties is challenging and fun. While Andrew
was Principal of New College at the University of Toronto during the

mid-seventies, we had a lot of practice entertaining large groups. So it was very easy in 1976 to arrange a large party at the Hougues Magues for its 100th birthday. It doubled as a birthday party for Andrew.

At that time I had not yet started keeping a farm diary, but even so I can remember much that happened. Close to 100 people came, family and friends, sometimes three generations. We installed an outhouse down by the big pond for the twenty or more people who camped in tents around the pond. We organized useful activities like building fences and clearing fence-rows of dead trees, and amusing activities like horseshoes (Norm McKibbon supervised that) and badminton to keep adult males and children occupied. "The ladies" helped prepare a lovely outdoor buffet—the table centre-piece was a model of the Hougues Magues made by Andrew's father—and the food was served in huge bowls borrowed from the New College kitchen. We all shivered while we ate because even though it was mid-July, it was windy and cold. On Saturday evening we held a dance at the Bognor Hall to which the whole community was invited. We even had fireworks afterwards.

On Sunday, just before lunch was served, an elderly guest arrived, driven to our farm by her family. Eager, smiling, dressed in Sunday best, she came out of the car towards Andrew and me. Not more than ten steps from the car, her smile dissolved into tears. Weeping, she returned to the car and was driven away. She was Dan and Sarah Morrison's only surviving daughter. What were the memories that brought such sorrow?

TWENTY-TWO YEARS LATER we had another party with the same number of guests, but much more lavish. At the end of May, 1998, Nigel and his fiancée Caroline Boushira told us they would like to get married the beginning of August at the Hougues Magues. They meant August, 1998, not August, 1999 as some of our friends assumed.

What a wonderful challenge! I had expected that Nickie's 1980 wedding was the only one I'd ever be much involved with, but here was a second occasion. With both the couple and the bride's parents living so far away in Montreal, I had the fun of making many of the arrangements; e-mail kept us all in constant communication.

There were three aspects to planning the wedding. The first was completely in the couple's hands—arranging who would officiate, choosing the guests, sending out the invitations, and deciding who would be in the wedding party and what would be worn. The second was practical. That included renting a tent, deluxe portable toilets and a dance floor as well as choosing tables, chairs, table linens, china, glasses and cutlery. Nickie provided two dark fruit-cakes for the three-tiered wedding cake which was decorated locally. A friend who knows Owen Sound inside out, Ernestine McKenna, advised us on caterers, florists and hairdressers. Andrew found a piper from Owen Sound on the Internet and two Toronto musicians for the wedding ceremony. We knew we wanted Peter Rissi to provide the dance music. In spite of the short lead time, everything was done.

The third initiative was the direct result of looking at the Hougues Magues and its environs with a critical eye rather than seeing it through our usual rose-coloured glasses. All of a sudden things that we'd been putting off demanded instant attention. The verandah and worn wicker furniture were patch-painted and broken screens replaced; rusted handles on screen doors got painted and external windowsills got properly cleaned; windows were washed and internal sills repainted; the front door got repainted and so did the screen doors. Curtains that I had made but left unhemmed were hemmed by Monique and me. The garden was put in a state of pristine weedlessness and major pruning of the trees in the garden was accomplished. Stone steps and paths were stabilized. Young Andrew painted wooden signs to direct people from the temporary parking lot to the "Wedding" and to the "WC." And because the summer of 1998, while never too hot, was so very dry, we even had a truck bring in about 6000 gallons of water, just to persuade the lawn to remain green.

ON THE MORNING OF the wedding, it was obvious the weather was going to be perfect all day. The Guernsey flag flew from our flagpole along with the Canadian Maple Leaf. Guests who'd arrived the night before picked flowers in the fields and, supervised by artist and friend Tamar Ehrlich, made garlands to decorate the wooden arch through which the bridal party would later emerge for the ceremony, led by the bagpiper. In the early afternoon, Nickie, her children, her mother-in-law and I, sat on the verandah wrapping pieces of wedding cake in tiny doilies tied with ribbon, all at the last minute to prevent them from being crushed.

Finally, after so much thought and planning, the event was about to begin. Our guests had parked their cars in the far-off parking lot and followed young Andrew's signs to "The Wedding." They had been welcomed at the gate and then assembled below the terrace where the ceremony would be conducted. The groom's party took its place and everyone waited. Suddenly all the guests turned around in unison to look southward. There in the flower-filled field beyond the house yard were Sigi and Walter Blaesi, Walter with his extra-long alpenhorn sounding a salute and Sigi ringing a huge brass bell from Switzerland. It was a magical beginning. Immediately this fanfare ended, the sound of the bagpipes could be heard from the woods to the northeast of the house, kilted piper as yet unseen. Just as planned, the piper came through the garlanded arch and then stood facing it to pipe in the bride and her attendants.

Reconciling the Jewish traditions of Caroline's family from Quebec with a secular service in a garden on a Saturday had not been easily accomplished. But a serene and eloquent Fred Miller conducted a service meaningful to all. Caroline's father and sister provided readings from the Old Testament and Nickie read a Shakespeare sonnet. The Ehrlichs brought a ketubah, part of a traditional Jewish wedding.

**Walter and Sigi Blaesi with alpenhorn and bell
at Nigel and Caroline's wedding.**

Afterwards, a very devout Catholic friend told us, somewhat to our surprise, that it was the most religious wedding he had ever attended. That he recognized the sincerity and authenticity in Nigel and Caroline's wedding ceremony greatly pleased us.

After the ceremony there was an informal reception on the south terraces, and more music as Walter sat on a rock and played his accordion. His music charmed our visitors from Quebec—and everyone else.

Finally it was time to go to the big white tent in the meadow to the west of the house. A small reception line was waiting for the guests who then proceeded through a specially contrived gap in the fence. On either side of the gap, the fence-posts were decorated with tulle streamers and flouncy yellow and white satin bows. A red carpet led on to the tent entrance flanked on each side by flower standards.

Tables for eight had been set up the day before, with floor-length yellow tablecloths and high-backed white café chairs. Each table had a fish-bowl centre-piece with floating flowers and candles, all assembled that morning with flowers picked in the fields and the garden—Sigi's as well as ours. Nigel, using computer graphics, had made attractive cards to list who would be sitting at each table. Gold ribbons and dried yellow roses provided by Nickie decorated the tent walls and the candelabra that flanked the head table. Unconventionally, the head table was occupied by the bride's and groom's families. There were two masters of ceremonies—one for the unilingual Anglophones, the second for the unilingual Francophones—but a surprising number of guests were bilingual.

Before dinner was finished, Peter Rissi and his musicians began playing and the dancing started. Guests had to cope with a slippery, not quite level dance floor. People slid, slipped and fell, causing gales of laughter, but no one got hurt. At least when we danced a hora, we were able to hold each other up.

We had gone to some trouble to get good fireworks—in fact many hours of trouble—but get them we did. At the end of the evening, a group of young men led by Michael went to the southernmost border of the farm and started setting them off, one at a time. The booming of the fireworks persuaded some to leave the tent to watch. What an extraordinary sight! The fireworks, seen from afar, appeared to be soaring upward to reach a full moon, floating high in the sky to the south of us. In the foreground, perhaps fifty feet from the tent, stood Caroline and Nigel alone, silhouetted against the moonlight and the fireworks, she with her white, full-skirted wedding dress, he in black formal attire. At that point, quite by chance, Peter started playing Gershwin's shiveringly beautiful song, *Summertime*. Totally serendipitously, one of Nigel's friends went up to the microphone and began to sing. It could not have been more perfect.

When the guests had been given their wedding cake and began their journey across the dark field back to their cars, they all carried giant sparklers. Our niece, Dianne Lyon, observed that her family's sparklers burned brightly until they reached their car, found their car-keys and opened the door. She quite mistakenly attributed this convenient phenomenon to her aunt's planning. It wasn't planned. It was just more serendipity.

⚬ ⚬ ⚬

BUT THERE ARE REASONS other than weddings to bring friends together. Almost every summer, often in late August, we will have twenty or thirty guests for Sunday lunch. It requires much less effort than having people for dinner. No other time of the week is quite as relaxed as the mood of a Sunday morning. If we are lucky, the day is warm and the garden can be enjoyed as well as the conversation. What more can be asked for than sitting under trees, enjoying a glass of wine, and gazing at verdant lawns and distant vistas?

For these events, the menu is always designed to be simple with as much preparation done in advance as is humanly possible. Some years we have barbecued hamburgers and sausages, other years served quiches, sometimes a ham. Always salads. But there is one dish that appeals to our guests more than anything else. When everyone is so focused on their cholesterol levels, it's a bit surprising that this is the dish they all want recipes for! And second helpings. A tossed green salad and a tray of sliced tomatoes garnished with black olives and fresh basil go well with this recipe.

Cheese and Onion Bread Pudding

The night before, remove crusts from one thinly sliced sandwich loaf. Arrange a single layer of slices in a greased 9x13 inch pan. Cube 12 oz Brie and grate 8 oz old cheddar. Chop 1 large red onion and prepare 2 tbsp chopped parsley. Beat together 6 eggs with 2 tbsp Dijon mustard and then beat in 3 cups cream (or milk). Spread half the cheeses, onion and parsley on the layer of bread. Pour one third of the egg mixture over the cheese. Arrange another single layer of bread on top of the cheese, and then spread the remaining cheese and onions evenly. Pour one half of the remaining egg mixture on top. Place the final layer of bread on top of the cheese (you will use an entire loaf) and pour the remaining egg mixture so that all the bread is moistened. Cover with plastic wrap and refrigerate until one hour before baking. Bake at 350°F for one hour, and let rest ten minutes before serving. This will serve eight to ten people.

After such a cholesterol-rich main course, fruit is the best dessert, either fresh fruit, or possibly pears poached in red wine with bay leaves. If the main course allows for a dessert with cream in it, there are three favourites we have used—each prepared with a minimum of fuss when you have more than a dozen guests.

Duncan Hines Chocolate Gala

Astonishing though it may be, the Baines' on occasion do use a cake-mix. My daughter taught me to, late in my cooking life! Even more astonishing is that our discriminating friends loved it.

Begin with a chocolate cake mix and make two nine-inch layers to serve 10 people. Put cakes on two serving plates and sprinkle each with icing sugar through a sieve. Allow guests to help themselves to scoops of ice-cream or spoons of whipped cream or both. The finishing touch, probably the only reason why people are so fond of this is:

Chela Haber's Chocolate Sauce

This recipe is proof that long after you lose contact with friends, recipes they gave you keep their memory alive. It also demonstrates that I live in two different worlds, one metric and one not. This recipe is metric because Chela was European. Her chocolate sauce is usually poured unsparingly over cake or ice cream, so for very large crowds you may end up tripling the recipe.

> Heat 1/4 litre water with 225 g white sugar to boiling.
> Mix a little of the hot liquid into 75 g cocoa which has been
> combined with 5 mL cornstarch. Pour in the rest of the
> hot liquid. Then return to saucepan and bring to boil. Remove
> from heat and add 125 mL whipping cream. Heat gently until
> it just comes to a boil.Serve warm.

But there are always people who prefer fruit and for them the following grape dessert is very appealing. It's so appealing that it's always sampled even by those who enjoy the chocolate cake.

Tamar Ehrlich's Chilled Green Grapes

It may be misleading to say this is quick to prepare. Removing the stems from sufficient grapes to serve a large group does take time. Monique and Nickie have done this for me many times. The quantities below will serve four as a main dessert, more for people who are just sampling.

> Wash and remove stems from 1 lb seedless green grapes
> which are firm and sweet. Dry on tea towels. Put in bowl and mix
> with 1 cup sour cream and the grated rind of one orange. Chill for
> several hours. Just before serving, mix in 1/4 cup brown sugar.

Tamar's recipe is just one of two fruit desserts that we enjoy very much. The second one should be made with blood oranges, but because they are usually not of very good quality in Toronto stores and are always extremely expensive, we use seedless navel oranges.

Janos Hrabovszky's Orange & Walnut Compote

When Janos makes this dessert, he cuts thin round slices of orange, leaving a tiny rim of white around them, which looks very nice, but can be difficult to eat if the diameter of the orange is larger than your mouth or your spoon. Instead, Andrew and I usually separate out the wedges of orange from the surrounding membranes.

> Wash and dry as many seedless navel oranges as needed. Depending on the size of the oranges, you may need one or two per serving. Pare thin slices of peel from all the oranges and chop finely. Use as little of the white pith as possible. Then finish peeling the oranges, removing all the white. Place sections or slices in serving bowl. Add peel. Just before serving, add brown sugar to taste and as much rum as pleases you. Sprinkle coarsely chopped walnuts on top and serve.

❧

OUR NEW YEAR'S EVE party is always very special. The core guests are two couples who have been coming for almost two decades and another couple who has joined us for the last decade. Others have come and gone. To me, it's wonderful that sometimes we are joined by the next generation—either our children or the children of other couples who come. Parties that bring together different generations are very special.

Usually only twelve sit at the table, but sometimes there are fourteen. All of us share two interests, namely entertainment and good food. To achieve them, our guests stop at nothing. Before we acquired a 4-wheel-drive vehicle, coming to this event required using skis or snowshoes to haul in party clothes, sometimes costumes, plus elaborate food and generous supplies of wine and champagne, often after dark had fallen. Andrew and I were used to this routine, but that our guests were willing to go along with it was quite something.

The evening begins with wine and hors d'oeuvres in the living-room starting about 7 p.m., sometimes delayed if our Toronto guests are late arrivers. Then we go on to a multi-coursed dinner which includes soup, a fish course, sorbet, a main course, salad, and dessert, with each couple assigned responsibility for one course. Dessert is rarely offered before 12:30 a.m., after we have saluted the arrival of the New Year.

The reason for dinner taking five hours or more, is that between each course, one couple is designated to provide some form of entertainment. Over the years, these New Year's Eve parties have had a number of themes. One year we all tried to evoke what life might have been like in Sydenham 100 years before. One guest read selections from a newspaper published then, taking the role of the head of the house reading the newspaper aloud to his family in the evening, informing them of what was going on in the world. Another couple performed popular songs of the period. And someone pretended to be the Treasurer of the County giving his annual report to council, which was indescribably hilarious. Another year the theme was Charles Dickens, and guests arrived dressed as favourite characters from his novels, performing skits related to their characters.

The theme for 1998-1999 was Oscar Wilde with excerpts from some of his plays, and a wonderful recounting of his aphorisms. To evoke Dorian Gray, Tamar Ehrlich, wearing a rubber mask that transformed her into a hideous old crone, arrived with a large oil portrait of herself as a young girl. For the beginning of the year 2000 we are planning to have everyone represent a favourite character from the last millennium. I would suspect the observers will have to identify who these characters are. Of course putting on skits, playing charades, singing songs and reading are all activities which were very much the norm in the 19th century when friends were entertained in private homes. It works extremely well, even at the end of the twentieth.

Our New Year's Eve celebration always ends with everyone making three predictions for the next year—predictions never made until after those from the previous year have been reviewed. They range from the flippant to who will win the next election in the United Kingdom, the U.S. or in Canada, to what wars will break out, to peace settlements that will or will not be reached, to who among our offspring will get married, to the stock market, the price of oil, the rate of inflation or the value of the Canadian dollar, to who will win the Stanley Cup. However, the older we get, the more the predictions are dominated by our expectations for our investments!

It is a great pleasure to us both that so many people enjoy being at the Hougues Magues.

Chapter 18

Reflections

A terrible swiftness of events seems the penalty
for having such a rich and happy life.

Entry from my diary June 28, 1979.

W E DID HAVE another life. In spite of all we did at the farm, more than three-quarters of our time was spent in Toronto where we both had busy careers. Since 1970 Andrew has been successively Principal of New College at the University of Toronto, Chair of his Department, Biochemist-in-Chief for Canada's largest hospital and finally, his term of office completed in the fall of 1999, Vice Dean Education in the Faculty of Medicine. All the while he has run a research laboratory and taught undergraduate and graduate students. In the same period, I completed my internship which had been delayed for ten years because of ill health, earned a Master's degree, and progressed through the ranks from lecturer to full professor at the University of Toronto.

We've also had our responsibilities to maturing children and to aging parents. Now with the exception of some long-lived aunts and uncles on both sides, Andrew and I are almost alone in the front row of those marching through their lives.

Being told in 1972 by physicians that I had one year to live, or more accurately, that I'd be dead in a year, like the threat of hanging, made Andrew and me focus our attention acutely on what was important in a life. I was told I had a lymphoma, the same disease that killed the Shah of Iran and Jacqueline Kennedy. Why would I now share such information? To bring home to others how much life can offer, how much can be accomplished, even after terrible news. A lot has happened since we bought the farm in 1970.

Obviously, most of our energy and attention was directed other than at the farm. Yet, as anyone knows who has read this far, our Sydenham experiences have been rewarding beyond description, diverse and sharable, and fun. The benefits to us have been enormous. We have gained new wisdom and new friends. Our physical labour has helped keep us more fit than we would otherwise have been. Too many Friday evenings Andrew's face looked drawn after a stressful work-week. By Sunday, he was restored physically and spiritually. When self-directed, physical work is good for the soul and body. At the Hougues Magues, there was refuge from controversy, conflict and disappointment. Anything that disturbed our lives in Toronto, became trivial, irrelevant and at least for a moment, forgettable at the farm.

Our friends benefited too. Some have stayed at the Hougues Magues when we were not there, and found renewal of spirit. Others have spent several days camping by our big pond. An elderly widower who stayed with us overnight joined us at breakfast saying it was the first time he had enjoyed uninterrupted sleep since his wife had died a year before. Another couple, both wounded from previous unsuccessful marriages, first came to "know" one another in our guest bedroom. Next morning, the woman confided to me that "it hadn't been great." Practice must make perfect because in spite of this inauspicious beginning, they recently celebrated the 20th anniversary of a very happy marriage.

But there is always a cost for any choice you make. In retrospect, I think the cost of incorporating a country home into our lives was less for us than it was for our children. We made our decision for ourselves but they didn't. Nickie and Nigel, as long as they were young, just came with us, because in our mind, their social needs had a lower priority than the family being together at the farm. They survived. As they grew older, they would stay in Toronto sometimes, though their friends were always welcome at the farm. As I watch our grandchildren growing up, I realize how much has changed. By the age of five they had busier weekend schedules than their parents. It would be a very rare weekend that one or other of them didn't have a party, sometimes two, to go to. If not parties, there are always sports, lessons and shopping to interfere with any routine escape from the city. Absent all those obstacles, there is an increasing tendency for the workplace to encroach on weekends. Everyone's free time is diminishing.

You can't have a meaningful relationship with a country home unless you recognize that you will be saying "no" to many invitations you receive for dinner on Saturday evenings, to say nothing of concerts and plays. Our Toronto friends indulge us, inviting us for Friday or Sunday, or a week-night. Never (hardly ever) on Saturday! But there were still many events and invitations we refused over the years to protect our weekends at the farm. We have observed others dealing with this problem—and many of those who bought properties similar to ours lasted five to ten years, and then decided they couldn't bear being pulled in two directions.

You do what you choose to do. Some choices inevitably preclude other opportunities.

❧❦❧

I WRITE A CHRISTMAS LETTER every year to friends now far away, friends like Lou and Janos, and every year as I finish the letter, I always have uncomfortable twinges. All the wonderful adventures Andrew and I, and the rest of the family have had and what's happened at the farm are described. It is such a painful contrast to the misery and social upheaval all around us all the time. We have two homes and others have none. Writing this book triggered the same unease.

We live in a "Gilded Age" where some are very wealthy and many more are very poor, and the very poor, especially in underdeveloped nations, are largely invisible. This was the theme of an article in the August 14, 1999 issue of *The Economist*, by Jeffrey Sacks. One example he gave is that of the pharmaceutical industry failing to address the health problems of poor nations. That industry doesn't see it to be in their economic interest to develop vaccines that poor countries will not be able to pay for. Rather, it is very much in their interest to develop more treatments for affluence-related heart disease in the Western world. His article triggered a chain of thoughts in me, examples of how we all wear blinkers most of the time allowing us to ignore what we choose to ignore.

On a recent summer evening, Andrew and I went for a walk in Yorkville, considered a major Toronto tourist attraction with its many boutiques and restaurants. The sidewalks are moderately wide but even so, we had to walk around large bags of garbage and piles of empty cartons in front of the stores. It smelled. It was disgusting. But the city fathers, and I suppose the merchants too, ignore this reality. With blinkers on they can proclaim: Yorkville is a big tourist attraction!

Other blinkering? Everyone knows air pollution is bad for your health. Air pollution is directly related to morbidity (illness), hospital admissions and mortality (death rates). Every Sunday evening when we return to Toronto, the city is lying under a mushroom cloud of yellow smog. We've been assured the yellowness has no significance. I don't believe it. Andrew and I know the air is fouled when we ride our bicycles home from the university during the evening rush hour. We know the air is fouled when we drive on highways and see the transport-trailer trucks belching black into the air every time they change gears. Blinkered, our politicians acquiesce to demands for more highways, more trucks, more cars—and fail to enforce effective pollution control.

I could go on and on. There are countless instances where the blinkered manage to ignore reality and prevent effective measures from being implemented. In the face of all that, what can one family do to change things? We chose the default option, doing what was within our power. We tried to educate our children well and to give them standards; we hope we are enriching the lives of our grandchildren; we support local merchants and hire local labour; we have our favourite charities and support the arts—all of which isn't very much help in the larger scheme of things. And, we still have two comfortable and well-loved homes when others have none. We too are blinkered.

⁂

THE NUMBER OF government grants we have received over the last three decades is amazing. Never did these grants pay for all the costs involved in any one project, nor should they have. We were just grateful that some of the costs were met by the grants—grants for removing elm trees and creating a pond, support for planting trees, subsidies on trees, a grant to install UFFI, another grant to seal it in, and a grant to fence the creek to keep out livestock. We were given expert advice about developing and managing our forest. As well there were property tax rebates for both the managed forest and the agricultural land. The tax rebates were properly restricted to the forest and pasture assessments. The assessment on the residential area was excluded from the rebate programs.

In all, about 10 different programs were involved. From a public policy point of view, was this a good thing? It's easy to say that those programs and others like them, contributed to the provincial debt. On the other hand, the virtue of these programs is that they were given to individuals who went on to do things they might not otherwise have done. While we were able to plant one or two thousand trees a year, we never could have planted tens of thousands. The grants we received resulted both in concrete outcomes (trees, increased water storage capacity in soil, and more diversity of wildlife to say nothing of reduced energy consumption) and in indirect benefits to the local economy. We hired experts to fell a few dangerous elm trees, hired help to build some fences, sold saw-logs to local lumber mills, and provided a supply of firewood for local woodcutters to market. The indirect help to the local economy also included support for local small business whether it was for the insulation and the subsequent sealing procedures, or for the ongoing purchases of fencing, spikes, tools and equipment, and the servicing of equipment.

In Ontario, these diverse grants are a thing of the past. The current provincial government is committed to reducing government services, which has resulted in the Ministry of Natural Resources being severely downsized. The Conservative government believes forest regeneration and pollution control is best left to industry. Foresters who used to work for the ministry are now entrepreneurs, private consultants to landowners, and the landowners pay them on a fee-for-service basis. One of the services the landowner needs, is advice as to which trees should be marked for cutting. The possiblity now exists that financially insecure foresters could be tempted to accept payments from industry, payments ensuring that the tree marking will be advantageous to industry, not necessarily what is right for the forest. It's understandable, but regrettable.

❧

As I wrote this book, one memory provoked another and it never seemed to end. These memories remind me that so much of what the farm is today, has happened with the help of others. A lot of what Oma did has already been mentioned, but she did so much more: picking apples and taking them back to the city to make them into Guernsey Gache-May-Lah for us to freeze and enjoy through the winter; making jam; embroidering cushions and wall hangings which are all around the house; being always so willing to do anything and everything. Margie Baines came to the farm much less frequently than Oma, but I can remember her raking topsoil before we seeded one of our new lawns. She enjoyed supporting particular projects like buying a special tree—a linden tree which survived Sydenham winters only a few years—or paying for new linoleum for the kitchen floor.

For many years, my father, Jan van Erk, skillful at pruning evergreens, looked after our cedar hedge assiduously—a "two-beer job" at least. He took pride in being a dripless painter and painted our many homemade wooden farm gates. His last job was a gate in the barnyard, which he painted only a few months before he died. The effort made him grey and I can remember him sitting exhausted in the living room afterwards, wearing a dreadful red shirt that he'd bought only because it was a bargain. His life in Canada had transformed him from a young and debonair violinist (he remained irresistibly charming and handsome to women of all ages, including my teen-age high school friends and much later, my mother-in-law) who had never "worked with his hands"—never done anything practical like pruning or painting or cabinet-making—into a successful businessman who still skated and rode a bicycle "no hands" in his mid-seventies. As for Barge, Andrew's father, he came, looked benignly on all around him, told jokes at the dinner table, went fishing with Nigel, sketched and departed. "Fish and guests start to smell after two days," he would always say.

Two Jewish families bearing candles, challah and white napkin, have brought Shabat (and Hanukkah) to the Hougues Magues—at home in our home. Over time we have invited graduate students from all over the world who were studying in Toronto, to Bognor. Usually living on very meagre budgets and trapped in the centre of the city, they seemed to find being in the country a special treat. Very often they would prepare dishes from their country in the Hougues Magues kitchen.

Early on, Ziggy Konrad, a gallant, moustached Polish airman who had been based in England during World War II, used to come and advise us about trees, especially Austrian pines which he loved, and then, with Nigel, he'd fly radio-controlled model airplanes on the front lawn. Ziggy couldn't do that any more with all the trees grown so tall. Mel Silverman helped Andrew put up fences in mosquito-ridden marshy areas years ago. It was Mel's daughter Sarah who got so excited about picking green beans. Barry Ehrlich helped build bridges and clear ski trails. Janos's niece Kriszta and her husband, Sandor Weinacht have tended bonfires in the best Hrabovszky tradition. Many others have helped build fences and prune the forest.

Was it an effort to impress his future in-laws that explained Michael's digging so many holes for fence posts while he was engaged to Nickie? His specialty now is tending bonfires.

For some of our guests, their memorable contribution to the farm was fine wine and fine food. One such donor was David Goldberg. Once, eager to be helpful when we were leaving the farm, he volunteered to shut the gate after the cars had driven through. He did shut the gate very successfully, but left himself on the wrong side of it and we unkindly continue to giggle! But people are always full of surprises. On a much later visit, after having serious heart problems, David skillfully kicked a soccer ball around with our grandson for at least half an hour on a very hot day. We knew he had been an amateur boxer and became a wine specialist. We never guessed he had been a good soccer player.

Then there were our wonderful neighbours, the McKibbons, the Carmichaels and the Emmersons. How often they came to our rescue when we were undecided or in trouble!

***

REMEMBERING ALSO MEANS recognizing change. So many people we remember are no more. Physical changes to house and land have been described but environmental changes have occurred too. At the farm, there has been a huge upsurge in wildlife around us, coyotes and deer particularly. There are far more wildflowers and wild grapes have become a nuisance. We have milder winters with less sunshine and less snow, and the increasing frequency of summer tornadoes is very noticeable. Beyond the farm, railway tracks have been converted to trails, the highways are increasingly congested and maniacal drivers drive 120 km per hour on two-lane highways where the speed limit is 80. (Thirty years ago, speed would always have been expressed in miles. Now we are metricized. And those of a certain age still flip back and forth between kilometres and miles, inches and centimetres, Fahrenheit and Centigrade, cups and millilitres, puzzling our grandchildren enormously.) Back in the city, there is ever more dense pollution and decreasing civility.

Marked differences since 1970.

A FAVOURITE TIME at the Hougues Magues for us is about 5:30 in the afternoon on a fine summer day. We sit with a drink on the verandah in our comfortable wicker chairs. The sun, slanting in from the west, casts such a warm and glorious light on the flowerbeds. If we have no visitors, it is very quiet—the quiet is a presence, felt physically, almost heard. Only the birds make any sound. It's much too beautiful to want to read. We overdose on serenity hoping it will last us through the week.

At the end of the day, serenity reigns on the verandah.

The fifth volume of Leonard Woolf's autobiography is titled *The Journey not the Arrival Matters* (The Hogarth Press, London. 1969). This book is our journey and it's the journey that was important—a journey with so many people, doing so many interesting things. The Anglican Book of Common Prayer instructs us to praise and magnify the Lord. But Andrew and I are agnostics. Is there a paradox? An irony? We have cared for the land a supreme being may have made. We have respected that which mankind hath wrought, displaying a respect for humans a supreme being may have created. Indirectly, we may be praising and magnifying the Lord just as the Book of Common Prayer instructs.

In the first few months after I had the lymphoma diagnosis back in 1972, I struggled with the fatigue associated with radiotherapy and with the shock of the dreadful prognosis I'd been given. Andrew told me I should write. So I wrote an essay to ease my soul. It ended with the conclusion that the act of living requires loving, being loved and doing. Twenty-eight years later I still believe this to be true. Or as they would say in Sydenham, "It *is* so."

ODE TO SYDENHAM

The poem below was included in *The History of Sydenham Township, Volume II 1967-1998*. It was written by Doreen and Robert (Bob) Tuck who live on the sideroad just north of our farm. Andrew calls them the Bards of Bognor, a title they certainly deserve. Bob is the fourth generation of Tucks to live close to the fifth line.

There's a place up in Grey County –
Up next to Georgian Bay –
Where the cold spring water sparkles
In the streams where fish do play.
There are picturesque hills and valleys,
Numerous beaches, coves and bays.
It is known as Sydenham Township –
So unique in many ways.

From the bluffs, plateaus, and ridges,
What a view on bright clear days.
There's the several miles of shoreline –
All the length of Georgian Bay.
There are forests of soft and hard wood,
Famous creeks – their names will stay.
There are lakes, and two named rivers –
The Bighead and North Spey.

When the early pioneers settled
Hardship was the price to pay.
They were helped by friendly natives
When in trouble or lost their way.
But the pioneers of Sydenham Township
Determined that they would stay,
And many of their descendants
Here remain to this very day.

There were Scottish, Irish, English,
And yes, many others too.
There were blacksmiths, masons, tradesmen –
With their many jobs to do.
They cleared the land for buildings
And fields to grow their food.
They built their roads and bridges,
Their schools and churches too.

Their Post Office was important,
As were mills and shops and stores,
In Annan, Woodford, Bognor,
And Leith down on the shore.
There were Hoath Head, Johnson, Balaclava,
Bothwell's Corners and Barryowen,
There were Silcote, Morley, Rockford
Many have now come and gone.

The pioneers of Sydenham Township
Helped build what it is today
And there still remains the challenge
To have it kept that way.
If you live in Sydenham Township
It's a place where you want to stay –
With the picturesque hills and valleys
And the view of Georgian Bay.

Regional Distractions

Getting there:

THE CLOSEST CITY to Sydenham Township is Owen Sound which is about a two-and-a-half hour drive from Toronto. Regular bus service is available from Toronto. From Lester Pearson International Airport it is about a two-hour drive, and limousine service is available. However, cars cannot be rented in Owen Sound, at least I couldn't in July, 1999, so anyone arriving by rail or by air would be wise to rent a car in Toronto. Owen Sound has its own airport. It also has a large well-equipped marina for anyone sailing the Great Lakes. To properly enjoy the environs, a car is required.

Staying there:

EXCELLENT HOTELS and motels are available in Owen Sound, although during special events they may well be fully booked. Appealing Bed and Breakfasts are available not only in and around Owen Sound, but also around Bognor. Extensive camping facilities are available at the Cape Croker Reserve.

Eating there:

THERE ARE MANY RESTAURANTS in Owen Sound but two are particularly good: Marketside and The Grey Heron. If you want more upscale restaurants, the closest is the Backstreet Café in Meaford, which is excellent and many more are available as you head east to Collingwood. Heading that way, the highway allows you to see apple country to the south and the shore of Georgian Bay to the north.

Special events:

The annual Salmon Spectacular draws many visitors and so does Summer Folk Festival when literally thousands come to enjoy traditional and contemporary folk music performed by groups from all over North America and beyond. It is held at Kelso Park, just at the periphery of Owen Sound on the shores of Owen's Sound.

Special facilities:

The Tom Thomson Memorial Art Gallery is a wonderful gallery on the bank of the Sydenham River, with an impressive permanent collection. It hosts excellent special exhibits thanks to a series of very competent curators. In addition, the gallery shop sells well-designed local crafts of the highest calibre.

The Owen Sound Public Library owes its grandeur to Andrew Carnegie. Spacious, well equipped, and with superb staff, it is the place to go if you want good reading, or background material on the region.

The Billy Bishop Heritage Museum which houses many World War I and II artifacts is close by.

The County of Grey/Owen Sound Museum is a superb facility, telling the story of the local history extremely well. It displays an 1845 log cabin, a 1900 log house and a 1920 farmstead. It also holds special events throughout the year which are always very enjoyable.

Harrison Park offers a lovely setting for a picnic, walking trails, interesting species of trees, birds, and a pleasant restaurant.

Local Attractions:

Scenic Caves.

Waterfalls, especially Inglis Falls.

Keady market – a true country market held every Tuesday, featuring as many as 200 vendors and three livestock sales rings.

Sydenham Auction Sales which sometimes are held on farms and sometimes at the auction building just off Highway #26 near the Sydenham Township Building.

Diverse fairs.

Cape Croker Reserve where you can visit a pow-wow (featuring drumming and dancing) in the summer.

Outdoor Activities:

Bicycling along the railway line from Meaford eastward.

Hiking along the Bruce Trail which follows the Niagara Escarpment 740 km from Niagara Falls to Tobermory at the tip of the Bruce Peninsula.

Golfing on seven local courses.

Cross-country skiers will find a network of trails in Sydenham while downhill skiers can enjoy the hills close to Collingwood.

Deer hunting season is in the fall. People also take coon hunting very seriously in the area. Coyotes have become such a nuisance for sheep farmers that they can be hunted with no limit.

Horses are available for hire.

Fishing is excellent both in the Bay and on the rivers: Chinook salmon, rainbow trout, lake trout and brown trout.

Naturalists may enjoy bird watching, mushroom hunting, or exploring for orchids.

Snowmobilers have access to 3000 km of groomed trails.

Nearby Destinations:

Sauble Beach on Lake Huron has wonderful sand dunes. Because Lake Huron is shallow here, the water is much warmer than most beaches on Georgian Bay. It is a perfect place for children and sun-lovers.

Saugeen Reserve is another First Nations site, and it too has an annual pow-wow.

Wiarton is the first sizeable town north of Owen Sound. You can get there by driving along the shore road after leaving Owen Sound. On the way, if you like looking at gardens, stop in at Keppel Croft in Big Bay. There is a whole network of gardens in the area which can be accessed on the Web at http://greynet.net/~ruralgardens. Wiarton has a number of special events during the year, wonderful swimming facilities and lovely scenery.

Fathom Five National Park at the tip of the peninsula offers 20 historic shipwrecks for underwater viewing.

Further afield:

It's well worth driving north up the peninsula to Tobermory, turning off the main road to visit the shore line communities as you go. A major reason to stop is to visit Larkwhistle, an interesting garden near Dyers Bay. On the highway there are several antique shops which can be fun to visit. Just before you get to Tobermory (where you could pick up the ferry for the almost two-hour trip to Manitoulin Island with its beautiful scenery and annual pow-wow), stop in at Cyprus Lake—wonderful for both hiking and camping. The high-cliffed shoreline is stunningly beautiful, the water Mediterranean turquoise.

The communities that extend south from Sauble, along the Lake Huron shore, are well worth visiting. Bayfield, Goderich and Southampton are particularly interesting with excellent restaurants, nicely restored streets and parks, and interesting shops. Grosvenor House in Southampton is an unusually good restaurant.

Going further south and west, it's about two hours' drive to Stratford, home of Canada's premier summer theatre offering fare to suit different tastes—Shakespeare, to Gilbert and Sullivan to Broadway musicals. It's in full swing from May to October. As well as premier theatre, it also offers premier restaurants.

ACKNOWLEDGEMENTS

The following people are much to be thanked for their help.

Andrew Armitage

Bob Bennett

Sigi Blaesi

Ruth, Lloyd & Ivan Carmichael

Anne Collins

Norah Egener

Don Emmerson

Jim Fulford

Elizabeth Gillies

Bill & Bev Harris

Marg Howard

Penny Hozy

Joan Hyslop

Pliny Loucks

Orla Manning

Frieda McKibbon

Richard and Betty Murdoch

Harris Oakes

Ben Redman

Peter Rissi

Paul Rush

Peter Russell

Jane Somerville

Jim Thomson

Robert & Doreen Tuck

Alexander Von Gernet

George Yost

Andrew, Nickie and Nigel have all nudged my memory, and Andrew has graciously put up with a wife foolish enough to try to write a book quickly. As for Monique, she is a phenomenal proofreader.

Sources

Armitage, A.   *Owen Sound: Steamboat Days.*
                              Erin: The Boston Mills Press, 1981.

                              *Owen Sound: The Day The Governor Came to Town
                              and Other Tales.* Cheltenham, Ontario:
                              The Boston Mills Press, 1979.

                              The Bruce Peninsula Explorer.
                              Owen Sound: Ginger Press, 1994.

Arthur, E. and   *The Barn, A Vanishing Landmark in
Witney, D.   North America.* Toronto: A&W Visual Library.
                              M.F. Feheley Arts Co. Ltd., 1972.

                              *Bognor Community Centre, Official Program,
                              May 2, 1958.* Produced by The Meaford Express
                              printers and publishers.

Brockman, C.F.   *Trees of North America: A Guide
                              to Field Identification.*
                              New York: Golden Press, 1968.

Bruce-Grey   *The Orchids of Bruce & Grey.*
Plant Committee.   (Owen Sound Field Naturalists).
                              Owen Sound: Stan Brown Printers Ltd, 1997.

Chapman, L.J. and   *The Physiography of Southern Ontario.*
Putnam, D.F.   2nd ed. Toronto: University of Toronto Press,
                              1973.

Davidson, T.A.   *A New History of Grey County.*
                              Owen Sound: Grey County Historical Society,
                              1972.

Eaglesham, L. and   *Born Running: Reminiscences of Mary Howell.*
Gatis, S. (eds)   Wiarton: Colpoy Creek Books, 1997.

Foger, H.   *Mit dem Mond Leben 1999.*
                              Munich, Germany: W. Ludwig Buchverlag GmbH,
                              1998.

Garry, J.P.   *Georgian Bay – An Illustrated History.*
                              A Boston Mills Press Book. Toronto: Stoddart, 1992.

Gentilcore, R.L. and   *Ontario's History in Maps.* For the
Head, C.G.   Ontario Historical Series.
                              Toronto: University of Toronto Press, 1984.

Good, C.   *On the Trail of John Muir.*
                                  Edinburgh, Scotland: Luath Press, 2000.

Graham, W.J.   *Greenbank – Country Matters in*
                                  Nineteenth Century Ontario.
                                  Peterborough, Ontario: Broadview Press, 1988

Grindlay, T.   *A History of the Independent Telephone Industry*
                                  in Ontario. Ontario Telephone Service Commission,
                                  1975.

Hale, J.   *The Old Way of Seeing – How Architecture Lost*
                                  its Magic (And How to Get it Back).
                                  Boston: Houghton Mifflin Co., 1994.

Halpenny, F.G. (ed).   *Dictionary of Canadian Biography:*
                                  Volumes VIII (1851-1860) and IX (1861-1870).
                                  Toronto: University of Toronto Press.

                                  Historical Atlas of Grey and Bruce Counties Ontario.
                                  H. Belden and Co., 1880.
                                  Stratford: Cumming Publishers, 1975 & 1980.

                                  History of Sydenham Township. Centennial Project.
                                  1967. Joint project of the federal and provincial
                                  governments, the Sydenham Township Council,
                                  and the Township's Women's Institutes.
                                  Owen Sound: Richardson, Bond and Wright Ltd.

                                  Indian Treaties and Surrenders from 1680
                                  to 1890 in Two Volumes.
                                  Printed by S.E. Dawson, Printer to the
                                  King's Most Excellent Majesty. Ottawa, 1905.

Jameson, A.B.   *Winter Studies and Summer Rambles.*
                                  Talman, J.J. and Murray, E.M. (eds).
                                  Toronto: Thomas Nelson, 1943.

Langton, H.H. (ed).   *A Gentlewoman in Upper Canada –*
                                  The Journals of Anne Langton.
                                  Toronto: Clark Irwin, 1950.

Marsh E.L.   *A History of the County of Grey.*
                                  Owen Sound: Fleming Publishing
                                  Company Ltd., 1931.

McIlwraith, T.F.

Looking for Old Ontario.
Toronto: University of Toronto Press, 1997.

Pirone, P.P.

Tree Maintenance. 5th ed. Toronto:
Oxford University Press, 1979.

Radcliff, T. (ed).

Authentic Letters from Upper Canada.
First published 1833.
Toronto: Macmillan, 1953.

*Reds of Grey. A Collection Apple Recipes
from Grey County Kitchens.*
Owen Sound: Ginger Press, 1995.

Reesor, E.B.B. and
Thomson, N.

Owen Sound on the Georgian Bay, Canada.
First published 1912; reprinted
Owen Sound: Stan Brown Printers, 1987.

Rempel, J.I.

*Building with Wood and Other Aspects of
Nineteenth Century Building in Central Canada.*
Rev. ed. Toronto: University of Toronto Press,
1980.

Ross, A.H.

*Reminiscences of North Sydenham:
An Historical Sketch of Annan and Leith.*
2nd ed. First published 1924.
Owen Sound: Richardson, Bond
and Wright Ltd., 1991

Rybczynski, W.

Home: A Short History of an Idea.
New York: Penguin, 1986.

Scardellato, G. (ed).

"Continuity and the Unbroken Chain:
Issues in Aboriginal History of Ontario."
Journal Ontario Historical Society,
Volume XCII. Spring, 2000.

Schmalz, P.S.

The History of the Saugeen Indians.
Ontario Historical Society Research
Publication No. 5, 1977.

Sydenham Township
History Seekers.

*History of Sydenham Township. Volume II
1967-1998.* Owen Sound:
Stan Brown Publishers, 1998.

Topp, E. and
Howard, M.

*More Put a Lid on It!
Small-Batch Preserving Year Round.*
Toronto: Macmillan Canada, 1999.